More Youth Retreats ▽

Creating Sacred Space for Young People

More Youth Retreats ▽

Creating Sacred Space for Young People

Aileen A. Doyle

Saint Mary's Press
Christian Brothers Publications
Winona, Minnesota

In Dedication to ▽

Mary, our Blessed Mother,
on the feast of the Visitation, 31 May 1989

In Honor of ▽

Tom and Lenore Becker,
my godparents and maternal grandparents

The publishing team for this book included Robert P. Stamschror, development editor; Mary Duerson Kraemer, copy editor; Rita Rae Kramer and Gary J. Boisvert, production editors; Brooks Bentley, illustrator; and Mary Abel & Associates, Inc., cover designer; pre-press, printing, and binding by the graphics division of Saint Mary's Press.

The acknowledgments continue on page 122.

Copyright © 1989 by Saint Mary's Press, 702 Terrace Heights, Winona, MN 55987-1320. All rights reserved. No part of this book may be reproduced by any means without the written permission of the publisher.

Printed in the United States of America

Printing: 6 5 4 3 2

Year: 1994 93 92

ISBN 0-88489-223-9

Contents ▽

Foreword 6
Introduction 7

Part A: Retreat Preparations
1. Taking Time for Reflection 10
2. Tips for Successful Retreats 14
3. Training Retreat Staff Members 19

Part B: One-Day Retreats
4. Come, Let Us Return to the Lord:
   A Parent-Teen Lenten Retreat 30
5. We Are Christ's Hands:
   A Discipleship Retreat 38
6. Lean on Me: An Eighth-Grade
   Graduation Retreat 45

Part C: Two-Day Retreats
7. Prepare the Way of the Lord:
   An Advent Retreat 52
8. Change My Heart, O God:
   An Alcohol and Drug Abuse
   Prevention Retreat 65

Part D: Three-Day Retreat
9. The Lord Is My Shepherd:
   A Spiritual Direction Retreat 76

Part E: Four-Day Retreat
10. Standing on Holy Ground:
    A Camping Retreat 90

Part F: Retreat Follow-ups
11. An Afternoon Gathering 104
12. An Evening with Parents 108
13. An Evening Potluck 111

Resources 113

Appendix: Eucharistic Liturgy Preparation 117

Acknowledgments 122

Foreword ▽

Over the past decade, the Church has outlined and developed a comprehensive approach to ministry with youth. This holistic approach recognizes the social, personal, familial, and spiritual needs of youth and the environments that affect their life. The ongoing evangelization and spiritual development of young people are indeed essential and integral to fostering and supporting their maturing faith. Retreat experiences are vital moments in these all-embracing evangelization attempts.

This retreat manual is an inspiring and creative effort to speak in a fresh way to the needs and hopes of young people, and to challenge retreat ministers to respond to their needs. God's word when proclaimed, celebrated, integrated, and lived in community is dynamic, life-giving, and calls for ongoing change and personal renewal. The possibilities for spiritual development and growth in faith are enormous when the energy and the giftedness of young people are brought into dialog with the vibrancy and richness of God's word.

More Youth Retreats is addressed to leaders in retreat ministry with youth. It is written to affirm, support, direct, and encourage creative initiatives in retreat ministry. The ideas, suggestions, and practical details offer youth retreat ministers a new opportunity to share the good news of Jesus and the wisdom of Christian spirituality in ways appropriate to the development, language, and symbols of youth. The goal of the retreat programs in this manual is to create a sacred space for the Lord and the retreatants to be together. In this environment, retreatants are encouraged to honestly explore their beliefs, attitudes and values, and are at the same time challenged to listen to other voices and experiences as they search for freedom and truth.

The book is an expression of the author's dream and conviction of the urgency to respond to youth. Once again, Aileen Doyle speaks to the heart and calls us to the excitement and challenge of sharing life with young people. She shows how youth and adults can work together in their efforts to live and spread the good news. Aileen is well worth listening to, you who know the hunger and hope of the heart of young people.

Sr. Edith Prendergast, RSC
Director of Religious Education
Archdiocese of Los Angeles
Feast of the Epiphany, 1989

Introduction ▽

Recently, I asked my eleven-year-old niece if she knew what a retreat was. She confidently assured me that she did know. She recalled that her friend had participated in a retreat once. He had told her that it was boring because the retreatants had to be quiet and pray a lot. With all the work I have done with young people, I was disappointed to hear that my niece had not heard of the positive retreats experienced regularly by many young people. My experience working with young people in retreat settings has convinced me that they can, and often do, have affirming and energizing retreat experiences.

During my four years at the Christian Brothers retreat house in Saint Helena, California, retreats were provided for more than eight thousand young people. I wrote my first retreat manual, *Youth Retreats: Creating Sacred Space for Young People,* to share those ingredients that I found make retreats enjoyable and growthful experiences. I wrote this second retreat manual with the same intent—to share with you additional retreat programs that are effective and designed with the needs of young people in mind.

In *More Youth Retreats,* I present seven retreats, three follow-up programs, and guidelines for training retreat teams. For each retreat program presented in this manual, **the goal is to create a space for the Lord and the retreatants to be together.** The intent is to provide a safe environment that invites and encourages the retreatants to honestly explore their beliefs, attitudes, and values. At the same time, the retreatants are challenged to examine various sides of an issue, to listen to other perspectives and experiences, and to continue their search for truth.

Chapters 4, 5, and 6 are one-day retreats. Chapter 4, "Come, Let Us Return to the Lord," is a Lenten program for parents and their teenaged children. Chapter 5, "We Are Christ's Hands," calls to discipleship eleventh and twelfth graders.

Chapter 6, "Lean on Me," is an eighth-grade graduation retreat.

Chapters 7 and 8 are two-day retreats. Chapter 7, "Prepare the Way of the Lord," is an Advent retreat for eighth, ninth, and tenth graders. Chapter 8, "Change My Heart, O God," is an alcohol and drug abuse prevention retreat designed for high schoolers of any age.

Chapter 9, "The Lord Is My Shepherd," is a three-day spiritual direction retreat designed for mature eleventh and twelfth graders who want a deeper religious experience.

Chapter 10, "Standing on Holy Ground," is a four-day camping retreat designed for high schoolers of any age.

The three retreat follow-up sessions are designed to help retreatants keep alive resolutions made during retreats. They also provide an opportunity for retreatants to gather again to renew friendships.

The first of the three retreat follow-up sessions is a two-hour afternoon program designed for the retreatants to meet after school. The second is a three-hour evening program for the retreatants and their parents. The third follow-up session is a five-and-a-half-hour evening potluck for the retreatants.

These programs need to be considered and adapted in light of the *facilities* being used, the personalities and needs of the *retreatants,* and the staff members' availability, personal styles, and experiences. Be creative in using these retreats. You might want or need to shorten or lengthen them. You might want to intensify them by adding activities or lessen their intensity by subtracting activities. You might even mix activities from the various retreat programs to create your own special retreats.

May God bless you and the retreats you direct.

Part A ▽

Retreat Preparations

1 ▽

Taking Time for Reflection

The retreat programs in this book flow from my beliefs about young people. Likewise, the way you conduct these retreats will be affected by your beliefs about young people. To help you better understand the programs, and to stir your reflection, I want to share my beliefs with you about personal wellness, personal sacredness, being social and separate, family influence, and youth retreats.

Personal wellness

I believe that God created each person with the capacity to enjoy life—to have a personal wellness. I believe, likewise, that God invites each young person to a way of life that will lead her or him to personal wellness.

Personal wellness comes about as a result of personal growth that maintains a healthy psychological, physical, and spiritual balance. These dimensions of a person are interrelated. A disruption or a lack of growth in one dimension has an effect on the others. All three dimensions need to be attended to and nurtured.

Psychologically, the young person is trying to establish identity, a language for expressing and communicating self, and a sense of belonging based on self-worth. This effort usually includes a struggle to maintain close relationships while establishing an individual separateness. Although the family and parents are important to the young person, there is a move toward independence. At the same time, peer relationships take on new significance and compete for the young person's time and attention.

The retreat programs in this book respond to the psychological growth needs of the adolescent by providing the following:
- themes related to adolescent concerns
- values-clarification opportunities
- a chance to explore vocational issues—personal, social, and occupational choices
- opportunities to learn social skills
- opportunities to deepen relationships—God, self, family, friends
- opportunities to learn and practice communication skills
- affirmation of personal talents and giftedness

The young person is also growing *physically.* Physical growth during the beginning stages of adolescence usually brings about hormonal changes that prompt increased energy, spurts of body growth, erotic and aggressive impulses, mood swings, and impulsive behavior. Unless extreme or bizarre these characteristics are normal.

Physical growth needs of the young person are met in the retreat programs by the following:
- adequate recreation
- adequate rest
- nutritional meals and snacks

Spiritually, the young person is moving toward an appropriation of religious beliefs and practices. This effort involves an honest search for the truth. Many young people feel comfortable in their relationship with God. They might, however, struggle in trying to find meaningful ways of belonging to the church community. Young people desire to share and discuss faith matters with peers, usually in private but also publicly when encouragement and a safe environment are present.

Spiritual growth needs are met in the retreat programs by providing the following:
- a nonthreatening environment in which to explore personal beliefs and time to do so
- a variety of prayer experiences
- time to learn about the Christian heritage
- consideration of the beliefs and values of the Catholic tradition
- thought-provoking spiritual reading
- reconciliation services
- eucharistic liturgies

Particularly important for meeting the spiritual needs of young people is a retreat that is oriented toward building community. The retreat activities encourage knowing God more deeply through interactions with others. The adolescent retreatants experience God not only in their relationships with their friends but also with their parents and other family members through the parent-teen retreat and the follow-up program.

Remember that the young people to whose spiritual growth we minister were born after Vatican Council II. I like to think of them as the first generation of a new Church. Our youth are the first generation since the Council of Trent (1545–1563) to experience and be taught ritual, liturgy, prayer, sacraments, service, and Christian community with an emphasis on personal participation. At times this new emphasis confuses young people. Some of them might be in a parish that is progressive and has this emphasis, while the neighboring parish might be quite conservative. A historical perspective can be very helpful to them as they struggle for identity in a Church that is, itself, growing and changing. I challenge them to take an active part in the direction our Church moves in the future.

Certainly, it is necessary to keep in mind, especially when your retreatants cover a range of ages, that all young people develop psychologically, physically, and spiritually at different rates. Do not simply stereotype all young people or presume that all are in the beginning stages of development. As young people mature, growth can be seen in all three dimensions. Their responses to adults and adult values may begin to reflect a new objectivity, and they may begin to internalize parental values. Preoccupation with their body and self decreases. An increase in emotional and intellectual capacities, along with a new confidence in self and trust in God, results in better mental and emotional balance. Be on the lookout for these signs of growth toward personal wellness in young people and support and affirm them.

Personal sacredness

A second belief and value I hold about young people is that each is sacred and worthy of respect. Virginia Satir, a noted family therapist, describes an approach to this sacredness in *Helping Families to Change* (New York: Jason Aronson, 1975):

> I believe people are like flowers, and flowers grow because they have sunshine, fertilizer, and water. I have yet to find a plant that would grow by issuing the edict, "If you don't bloom, I am going to beat you." As you know, plants do not respond very well to that. In fact, such treatment can be fatal. I also know that a plant sometimes becomes too heavy to bear its own weight, and I then have to put in a stake to help hold it up until it grows strong enough to support itself. This is my model, and everything I do is related to how I can help the human being open up and blossom. (P. 166)

My belief in and value of the sacredness of each person, and the respect due to them, especially affects the training program for the staff members. Staff members are trained to create an atmosphere that allows for differences, provides for honest, direct communication, affirms gifts and talents, and encourages personal responsibility.

Encouragement of personal responsibility deserves special notation because it does convey respect, and the opportunity for such encouragement frequently occurs during a retreat. In encouraging personal responsibility in young people, I do not impose my convictions on them but rather nurture the growth of their own. Decisions that lead a person to his or her full potential can be made only by that individual. There may be times when young people need assistance. Like Virginia Satir's young plant, they at times may be too heavy to bear their own weight. But this is a temporary process, and eventually they must stand on their own. To know when and how much to assist a young person in making personal decisions is particularly important.

Being social and separate

A third belief I hold is that by nature we are both social beings and separate beings at the same time. I believe that while persons cannot fully function when dependent on others, they cannot fully function when independent of others. Interdependence is the ideal and most growth-producing situation.

In an interdependent relationship, two individuals relate as persons whose identities and self-worth are individual and unique but who share and enrich each other in their differences. These retreat programs provide opportunities for nurturing both the individual dimension and the social dimension of the young people. Community activities such as communal prayer, sharing of meals, and small-group discussion are balanced with individual activities such as individual prayer, quiet time, and journal writing.

Family influence

I believe that the family is the single greatest influence on an adolescent. Young people tend to unpack a lot of "family baggage" at a retreat. It is essential that retreat ministers listen to, and then build on, the positive aspects and strengths the retreatants have received from their family. Work within the frames of reference and beliefs of the retreatants' families as much as possible. Take advantage of any preretreat or postretreat connecting with the family to strengthen family relationships.

Youth retreats

Finally, I believe that a youth retreat is a sacred space where the young person and the Lord can be together. As a retreat minister, the goal is to create an environment—a sacred space—so that the Lord and the retreatant can meet. This responsibility is best carried out by planning and conducting a well-prepared retreat—a retreat appropriate for young people. Responsibility for a retreatant's meeting and being with the Lord is between the two of them. No matter how hard we try, we cannot make that happen, but we can create the space for it to take place.

In creating the space for the Lord and the retreatant to meet, it is important to plan activities that take into consideration the trust level of the retreatants. There is a natural flow in the development of trust that takes place in any gathering of people. During the initial gathering there is a limited amount of trust; after a period of interaction the trust level increases and bonds are formed that challenge the retreatants to share.

This flow is normal and similar to a river flowing downstream. When rocks, fallen trees, and other debris are in the water, the flow of the river is impeded. However, when all of the debris has been removed from the river, the flow is more fluid.

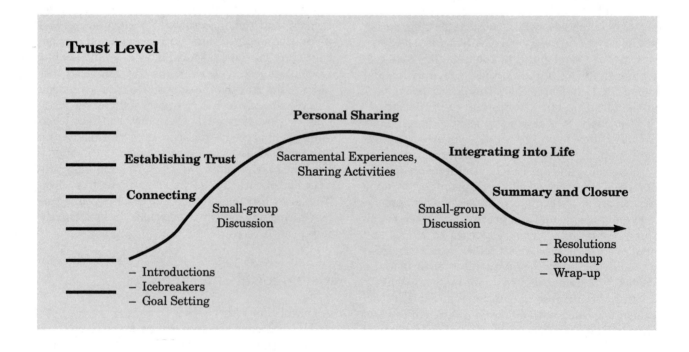

The same is true on a retreat. The task of the leaders is to choose activities that enhance the natural flow that is already taking place and to remove any obstacles that might impede the flow.

At the beginning of the retreat, trust is low. Activities are planned to help the retreatants connect with each other. Activities such as icebreakers, introductions, and goal setting help during this connecting time.

When the retreatants begin to share with one another, the trust level begins to increase. Activities that increase the level of trust are appropriate at this time. These activities include structured sharing of personal concerns.

After a meaningful retreat experience, it is important that the retreatants have the opportunity to integrate what they learned or gained from the experience into their daily life. For instance, if sharing with a retreat partner results in building trust, the characteristics of trust-building sharing could be named so the retreatants could use these in their relationships in general.

At the end of the retreat or discussion, it is important that the retreatants have some closure on the activity. This might be as simple as offering a closing comment that includes feelings or insights about the experience. Closure might also involve a decision regarding an action that could improve a particular relationship.

Being aware that this natural flow of trust is developing and taking steps to enhance it (through connecting, establishing trust, personal sharing, integrating learnings into daily life, and closure) will add to the quality of the experience for the young people.

2

Tips for Successful Retreats

Details in advance

Retreat facilities: Make preparations for the retreat well in advance. Some retreat sites must be reserved one to two years ahead of time. Before reserving the dates, check the retreat facilities for conference rooms, a chapel, small-group meeting rooms, the number of bedrooms, recreational facilities, mealtimes and menus, and costs. Sometimes small retreat groups might have to share the facilities with other groups. Be clear in your agreement with the retreat site regarding exactly what rooms you will be using. Many retreat sites require a nonrefundable deposit to reserve dates. You will also be responsible for reimbursing the retreat site for any damages caused by carelessness or misconduct. With young people, something usually gets broken on a retreat. So choose a facility that is designed to accommodate, and withstand, young people.

Letter to parents: Compose a suitable letter to the parents, informing them about the retreat their son or daughter has signed up to attend. Make sure that the parents have the address and phone number of the retreat facility in case there is an emergency at home. A permission and medical-release form can be included along with this letter. (See sample 2–A, "Letter to Parents," and handout 2–A, "Permission and Medical-Release Form," at the end of this chapter.)

Sign-ups: When the retreatants sign up for the retreat, ask for a nonrefundable deposit. Deposits are a good strategy, even if the deposit is only five dollars. Some young people sign up for a retreat and then back out at the last minute. Having a nonrefundable deposit helps to lower the number of last-minute no-shows and encourages the participants to take ownership of the retreat experience. The deposit also can provide capital to purchase supplies for the retreat.

Transportation: Decide upon and arrange for transportation (bus or cars). Make sure maps are available for the staff members and the retreatants who are driving. Have a list of names of the people traveling in each car.

Retreat staff: I advise that there be at least one adult on staff for each ten retreatants. (The retreat on spiritual direction, chapter 9, requires at least one spiritual director for every four retreatants.) Staff members are responsible for supervising, leading large-group activities, and facilitating small-group discussions. If a priest is needed, select one who is comfortable with young people and can speak to them. Make arrangements with him for the dates and times of his services. Choose staff members early enough to allow time for their training. (See chapter 3 of this manual for guidelines for training staff members.)

Preretreat meeting with the retreatants: If possible, meet with the retreatants to help them prepare for the retreat. (If it is not possible to meet with them, send them the necessary information.) Explain the theme of the retreat and the type of activities they can expect. Explain what will be expected of the retreatants, such as the following:
- being on time for activities
- participating in all activities
- respecting the privacy of each person's bedroom
- not using alcohol or illicit drugs

Distribute a list of the things the retreatants are to bring on the retreat, such as clothing, musical instruments, medications, and other items that are listed for specific retreats. Include on the list the time and place of departure.

Collect the balance of payment and the permission and medical-release forms. Also finalize travel arrangements. Answer any final questions the retreatants might have about the retreat. Encourage the retreatants to prepare for the retreat by praying for its success.

Details during the retreat

Breaks: Consider having the staff take turns supervising the retreatants during break times. This enables all the staff members to get to know all the retreatants and allows time for other staff members to prepare for their next presentation if necessary. To discourage practical jokes involving people's belongings, the sleeping area should be a restricted area whenever it is not supervised.

Chapel: The chapel, if there is one, is an ideal location for the introduction and the prayer at the beginning of the retreat. Beginning a retreat in the chapel can help to build a prayerful climate for the rest of the retreat. The chapel, along with several other places, can be designated as a quiet area for reflection and can also be used for large-group presentations if necessary.

Cleanup: Many retreat facilities expect the retreatants to remake the beds and to clean the rooms before leaving. Time is set aside for this on the overnight retreats. Also encourage the young people to clean up after themselves after breaks and mealtimes.

Closedown: To help the retreatants get an adequate amount of rest on the overnight retreats, ask them to have their lights out twenty minutes after the last activity ends. It might be wise to have an adult staff member supervise the halls to assure cooperation. If a retreatant indicates a need to talk to someone during this time, schedule a morning meeting with him or her. Both the retreatant and the staff member will be better able to approach a problem after adequate rest.

Discipline: If rules have been broken by a few people (e.g., trashing a room), call the group together. Without singling out the individuals who broke the rules, name the inappropriate behavior. Ask for assistance if such things as cleaning up the area need to be done. Refocus the retreatants by reminding them of the purpose of the retreat. Ask for cooperation and state the consequences you intend to give for any more inappropriate behavior.

Then carry on with the scheduled activity. Be consistent in enforcing the consequences if the behavior occurs again.

Discussion guidelines: Start small-group discussions by establishing discussion guidelines using the following steps:
1. Ask the retreatants to identify what helps make a good discussion.
2. Have them formulate guidelines that will help in their discussions. Make sure that the guidelines include confidentiality, respect, no put-downs, honesty, and an attempt to participate by all.
3. List these guidelines on a piece of butcher paper or newsprint and hang them for all to see.

Emergencies: In the event of a medical emergency, a staff member should accompany the retreatant to the doctor's office or the hospital. Bring along the retreatant's medical-release form. Call the parents immediately and call the school if you are conducting a school-sponsored activity.

Eucharistic liturgies: Some of the retreats in this book include a eucharistic liturgy. Resources for planning a eucharistic liturgy are found in the appendix on page 117. If a eucharistic liturgy is not possible or is not the best option, celebrate with a prayer service. A prayer service can follow the structure of a eucharistic liturgy, beginning with the penitential rite, moving on to the liturgy of the Word, and concluding with a type of communion rite, such as the Lord's Prayer and the sign of peace. If you choose to have a prayer service instead of a eucharistic liturgy, the retreatants can still plan the readings, the petitions, the decorations, the music, and the like.

Facility guidelines: During the orientation, cover such things as the location of rest rooms, property boundaries, whom to notify in case of property damage, meal responsibilities, the location of medical supplies, and rules for the sleeping quarters.

Icebreakers: An icebreaker is an activity designed to help the retreatants feel at ease with one another. Icebreakers with directions are given throughout the book, but feel free to use any icebreakers with which you are familiar.

Journal: Consider compiling a booklet that contains the handouts, discussion questions, and some blank pages for journal writing. Put the retreat theme and date on the cover. This booklet can serve as a retreat memento as well as provide the retreatants with more structure during the activities.

Meals: After meals, have the retreatants stay in the dining room until announcements have been made. This prevents the retreatants from being unsupervised. An adult staff member should supervise the cleaning of tables.

Memento cards: A nice touch is to give the retreatants a memento card from the retreat. These can be purchased in religious gift stores. An example of this is a card with "Footprints" or the "Peace Prayer."

Music: Music is a valuable addition to any retreat program. It helps to bring the group together. Even people with little or no musical talent can participate in a group singing activity. Retreats offer many opportunities to use music. Music can be used during prayer services, icebreakers, recreation, liturgies, or as a fill-in if a meal is not ready on time. Consider using some contemporary songs. They can have an added advantage. For example, hearing one of these songs on the radio after the retreat can help the retreatant recall the retreat experience. Tuning in the radio stations that are popular with young people will help you select contemporary songs that will work with the theme of the retreat. A music guide is included in the resources section of this manual, pages 113–116.

Before the retreat, invite staff members or retreatants who play instruments to bring their instrument and help lead songs.

Organized recreation: When the weather is poor and the retreatants are not able to play any organized games outside, use some indoor icebreakers. If an adult staff member is not directing recreation, have an adult supervise the recreation area.

Photos: A good way to capture the retreat experience is by taking pictures. Prints and slides can be shown to the retreatants during the retreat follow-up, or pictures can be distributed as mementos.

Reconciliation: The Sacrament of Penance often can be a suitable and effective part of a retreat. However, if a celebration of the Sacrament of Penance is not possible or is not the best option, a communal penance prayer service can be held. Another option is to invite the retreatants to come to staff members to pray together for forgiveness or to simply talk about a particular concern.

Schedules: Time schedules are important but often need to be flexible. In retreats with a large number of participants, activities tend to take more time than in retreats with fewer participants. If you rearrange the times suggested on the schedule, note the retreat center's mealtimes. These need to be respected for the sake of the kitchen staff. Post the schedule in the dorm, the dining room, and the recreational areas.

Wrap-up: The wrap-up time is intended to put closure on the retreat experience. It also helps the participants to prepare to return to their family, school, and job. The leader of this activity might remind the retreatants of the retreat theme and challenge them to keep alive any commitments or resolutions that they have made as a result of the retreat experience. This is also a time to make any announcements, such as where a group picture will be taken and when the retreat follow-up will be held.

Materials generally needed for a retreat

Lists: an alphabetical list of retreatants' names (one for each staff member) and a list of the membership of any small groups that have been determined ahead of time (one for each staff member).

Writing supplies: index cards, a roll of butcher paper or a pad of newsprint, 8½-by-11-inch paper, pencils, and felt-tip markers.

Materials for a eucharistic liturgy: a chalice, a plate, bread, wine, water, an altar cloth, a purificator, a candle, matches, a Bible, the sacramentary, music books, and copies of the liturgy program. See also handout A, "Planning Sheet for Eucharistic Liturgy" on page 121. It can be reproduced and used for all retreats.

Medical supplies: antibiotic ointment, bandages, cotton balls, alcohol, aspirin, allergy tablets, cough syrup, remedy for poison oak and poison ivy, antacid tablets, an ice pack, and feminine sanitary napkins. Make sure to get any needed authorization for dispensing medications and bring along the retreatants' medical-release forms.

Recreational equipment: Basketballs, soccerballs, footballs, volleyballs, playing cards, board games, and the like.

Miscellaneous: stick-on name tags, a camera and film, a tape recorder and tapes or a record player and records, extension cords, a roll of masking tape and a scissors for each small group, trash bags.

Additional items to bring are listed in the "Materials Needed for This Retreat" section at the beginning of each retreat program. Handouts are located at the end of the chapters.

Sample 2-A

Letter to Parents

[Address]

[Date]

Dear **[name of parent or guardian]**:

This letter is to inform you that your son or daughter **[name of retreatant]** has signed up to participate in an upcoming retreat.

A retreat is a structured program in which the participants take time to prayerfully reflect on their relationships with God and other people. The retreat leaders are a team of men and women trained to work with adolescent retreatants. Activities include prayer services, large-group activities, and small-group discussions **[include reconciliation service and liturgy when applicable]**. I have listed below some specifics about this retreat program.

In order for your son or daughter to participate in this retreat, please return the enclosed permission and medical-release form to me at the above address by **[date]**.

The participants will have a preretreat meeting on **[date]** at **[time]**. During this meeting they will be encouraged to pray for the success of the retreat. I hope you will do the same as we prepare for the retreat and especially while the retreat is taking place.

Please call me if you have any questions or if I can be of any further assistance to you.

Sincerely,

[Your name]
[Title]

Theme of the retreat: _____

Location, time, and date of departure: _____

Location, time, and date of return: _____

Cost, including travel: _____

Retreat facility: [supply the name, the address, and the phone number of the facility.]

Permission and Medical-Release Form

I give my permission for my son or daughter to participate in the retreat on _____ sponsored by _____.
    (date)

Retreatant's name _____

Date of birth _____

Address _____

City _____ State _____ Zip _____

Home phone _____ Parent's work phone _____

In the event of an emergency in which medical treatment is required, I give permission to the retreat director to obtain the services of a licensed physician. I wish to be notified immediately in the event of any emergency.

Please be aware of the following medical conditions for my son or daughter:
_____
_____
_____
_____

Other comments: _____
_____

Family Physician

Name _____ Phone _____

Address _____

City _____ State _____ Zip _____

Signature _____
                      (parent or guardian)

Date _____

3

Training Retreat Staff Members

How to begin

The training of staff members is an extended process and an integral part of preparing for a retreat. It involves recruiting potential staff members; surfacing their interests, talents, and experiences; identifying the tasks to be done before, during, and after the retreat; choosing staff members; assigning tasks; training large-group presenters and small-group facilitators; and involving the staff in finalizing the retreat plans.

If you are choosing a team of people who have not worked together as a retreat staff, this training process might take as long as two months. Allow adequate time for individuals to prayerfully reflect on their reasons for working on the retreat, for considering the ministerial roles a retreat calls for, and for measuring the time commitment involved.

I recommend that you take a team approach in leading a retreat for young people. A team offers a variety of talents and experiences and is better prepared to respond to the variety of needs that young people have. If, however, you will be offering a retreat to a small number of retreatants and you will be working the retreat alone, help prepare yourself by reviewing steps 2, 3, and 4 in the training process that follows.

The chart "Training Process Timeline" contains a timeline and description that can be used for scheduling and carrying out the training process.

Description of training process

1. Recruiting: Two months before the retreat, recruit potential staff members. Invite reliable people from a variety of situations (men and women; young and not-so-young people; married people, single people, vowed religious, and clergy; people experienced with retreats and those who are not experienced) to help with the retreat. The primary qualifications of these people must be that they are interested in working on a retreat for young people and that they have positive relationships with young people.

After inviting these people to consider working on the retreat, ask them to fill out handout 3-A, "Questionnaire for Retreat Staff Candidates," and to prayerfully reflect on whether God is calling them to help on this retreat.

2. Informing: After you have gathered the questionnaires, call a meeting to inform all the potential staff members about the retreat. This meeting should take place one-and-one-half months before the retreat. During this meeting, give an overview of retreats, explain the retreat goals, the retreat schedule, tasks to be done before, during, and after the retreat, and ministerial roles. This time can also be used to clarify any questions the potential staff members might have. At the end of the meeting, invite the potential staff members to spend the next two weeks prayerfully reflecting on ministerial roles, tasks to be done, the time commitment, and their own talents and interests relative to the retreat. Ask them to notify you within two weeks if they are still interested in working on this specific retreat.

3. Preparing: One month before the retreat, determine the members of the retreat staff and call a meeting with them to prepare for the retreat. During this meeting, assign tasks by ability and interest and train people for large-group presentations and small-group facilitation.

After the meeting, the staff members pray for the retreatants and prepare for their assigned tasks. Staff who are preparing large-group presentations should meet individually with those persons who are helping them prepare.

4. Finalizing plans: Two weeks before the retreat, call a meeting to finalize arrangements. Details that need to be finalized include travel arrangements, staff needs for their presentations (handouts, tape players, etc.), and the completion of a medical-release form for each staff member—which is to be used in case of emergency (see handout 3–B, "Staff Member Medical-Release Form"). The team takes time to pray for the success of the retreat and for the retreatants.

Staff ministerial roles

During retreats with young people, the retreat staff often is challenged to carry out several ministerial roles. Saint Paul gives an important insight for people who are going to carry out these roles during a retreat. He reminds us that we are God's co-workers and that God is the one who gives the growth (1 Cor. 3:7–9). The ministerial roles that are most often called upon during a retreat are Christian-adult role model, faith witness, educator, counselor, and midwife.

It is not expected that each retreat staff member be an expert in all of these areas. Rather, it is a team of people with a variety of gifts and talents that will, together, be able to fulfill these roles. A presentation on and discussion of these ministerial roles is an important part of training the retreat staff. Descriptions and examples of the roles follow, with personal reflection questions relating to each role. The personal reflection questions are also contained on handout 3–C, "Reflections on Ministerial Roles," which can be distributed to the staff members for their continued use.

Training Process Timeline

Time	Task	Activities
1. Two months before the retreat	Recruit.	• List names of potential staff members. • Give out handout 3–A, "Questionnaire for Retreat Staff Candidates."
The retreat coordinator and potential staff members prayerfully reflect on the call to work a retreat.		
2. One-and-one-half months before the retreat	Inform.	• Call a meeting for the potential staff members to inform them about the retreat goals, the schedule, tasks, and ministerial roles.
Potential staff members prayerfully reflect on ministerial roles, retreat tasks, and specific ways that they might be able to help on the retreat.		
3. One month before the retreat	Prepare.	• Call a meeting to finalize staff assignments and to train staff for large-group presentations and small-group facilitation.
4. Two weeks before the retreat	Finalize plans.	• Call a meeting to finalize travel arrangements, clarify staff needs for their presentations, and announce the date of the retreat follow-up program.

Christian-adult role model

"Let us love in deed and in truth and not merely talk about it" (1 John 3:18).

Whether an adult or a peer, as a retreat minister you will be looked to as a Christian role model. You will be observed in regard to honesty, respectfulness, genuineness, and responsibility. Even though you do not hold yourself as a model, the retreatants will look up to you and notice your behavior. You will actually teach more by actions than by words. During a retreat, young people notice how staff members treat one another as well as how they treat the other retreatants. They quickly sense how men and women staff relate with each other. They observe how the younger staff members treat the older staff members and vice versa. The tone of staff interaction influences the tone of the entire retreat.

You will especially be watched in how you enforce rules that have been clearly presented to the retreatants. For example, I had the responsibility to discipline some students who had been using drugs during the retreat. Because the rules about this had been clearly stated at the beginning of the retreat, I had to take some action. One of the retreatants who had been using the drugs was extremely angry with me. I tried to remain calm. Yet I was concerned about doing the appropriate thing. I felt that sixty other people had opinions about what needed to be done. I felt a lot of stress knowing the final decision was my responsibility. I had to constantly reflect on my responsibility to communicate with this retreatant as well as monitor the manner in which I would do it. It took a tremendous amount of effort on my part to be respectful, honest, and responsible in the way I enforced the rules about drugs.

Reflection questions
1. How might I best model Jesus' way for the retreatants?
2. What kind of situations might be the greatest challenge to my being a Christian-adult role model for the retreatants?
3. Who have been Christian-adult role models for me?

Faith witness

"The Spirit God has given us is no cowardly spirit, but rather one that makes us strong, loving, and wise. Therefore, never be ashamed of your testimony to our Lord" (2 Tim. 1:7–8).

The role of faith witness asks that you be attentive to your own faith journey and share it with the retreatants. Sharing your faith journey with the retreatants will be mutually beneficial—to them and to you. You will gain needed perspective for your journey, and they will find the words and encouragement to articulate theirs. When personal disclosure takes place, it is important that it be respected as unique and valid. Young people need support and encouragement during their faith struggles. They need models that inspire them and give hope for the future. For example, in speaking to retreatants about my own relationship with God, I share an experience that helped me grow in understanding God in my life.

When I was twenty-one, my sixteen-year-old brother, Joe, died from injuries sustained in a car accident. I struggled through a period of grief, searching for consolation in my faith and in what religious education had taught me. One day I came across Psalm 13:

> How long, O God? Will you forget me forever?
> How long will you hide your face from me?
> *(Psalms Anew)*

I was amazed that the writer of the psalm had felt the same as I did and voiced for me what I was unable to say. This was a turning point that began my healing process. My understanding of God expanded to that of a loving presence within me who was there to comfort me during difficult times. And I realized that if the psalmist could speak honestly to God, then so could I!

Reflection questions
1. How have I been a faith witness to others?
2. Have there been times when prayer has helped me in being a faith witness to others?
3. In what ways do I see myself being a faith witness to the retreatants?

Educator

"Now then, teacher of others, are you failing to teach yourself?" (Rom. 2:21).

The role of educator in a retreat is to draw out and then lead the retreatants to a deeper understanding of what they previously learned. This often simply means presenting information using words and concepts that have concrete meaning for young people. For example, if topics like heaven, hell, and sin come up during a retreat, I relate them to the language and the concepts of love and friendship. I remind them that in John's first epistle we are told "God is love" (4:8). Because heaven is union with God, it can be envisioned as that oneness experienced in love and friendship. Hell would be the opposite—the experience of the loss of love through one's own fault. Continuing with this same analogy, sin is choosing to do those things that break down love and friendship.

Reflection questions
1. In what ways do I see myself carrying out the role of being an educator for the retreatants?
2. In what areas do I need some additional knowledge for carrying out the role of educator during the retreat?
3. How can I best translate into adolescent language the meanings of church belief and teachings for young people while remaining faithful to their truth?

Counselor

"Love is patient. . . . Love . . . is not self-seeking" (1 Cor. 13:4–5).

The role of counselor has a number of dimensions. At times you will serve as a sounding board by feeding back to the retreatants what you heard them say. At other times you will be a validator by letting them know that you understand what they are feeling and that this is normal. Often, you will be a guide by exploring with them issues involved in their decision-making. Sometimes you will need to be a shelter that protects them from revealing more personal information than they are comfortable in doing, especially during small-group discussion when peers may be pressuring for more disclosure.

Finally, in the role of a counselor you will need to know when and where to make a referral or to make required notifications. Some states require immediate notification to parents or authorities in cases of suspected suicide attempts or abuse. In all cases, if you have not been trained and authorized to work with situations such as anorexia, abuse, alcohol or drug dependency, pregnancy, and suicide attempts, you will need to refer persons to appropriate agencies.

For example, during a retreat I realized that a retreatant was suicidal. I was relatively new in the field and was very concerned for her safety. I knew this was beyond my expertise, yet I had to do something. So I picked up the phone and called the local crisis hotline number. I explained to the crisis counselor that I was working on a retreat and that one of the retreatants was suicidal. The crisis counselor was extremely helpful in instructing me about what to do. Eventually this retreatant was referred to a psychologist, and she received the help that she needed.

Reflection questions
1. What skills and experience do I have that will help me carry out the role of counselor during the retreat?
2. What kinds of counseling situations would I need to refer to an appropriate agency?
3. What are signs that new growth is taking place in another person?

Midwife

"If anyone is in Christ, he is a new creation. The old order has passed away; now all is new!" (2 Cor. 5:17).

The role of midwife at a retreat is to be present and to assist when new life and birth occurs. At a retreat it means encouraging the retreatant, in a skillful, gentle, and enabling manner, to go beyond stereotyped or old roles to a new way of living. For example, a couple years after my brother died, I decided to go on a retreat. I was struggling with a number of unresolved issues and mixed feelings. Emily, a Sister of Charity of Nazareth who directed the retreat, loved me when I did not feel lovable. Emily was direct, honest, and challenging. She was gentle and faithful.

During this retreat, a new spirit began to grow in me. A lot of healing took place. I felt as if I were becoming a new person. Emily was able to discern this newness in me, and her gentleness and directness helped me to name it and give it expression. Emily acted as a midwife by coaching me, affirming me, and loving me as I gave birth to a new beginning in my life.

Reflection questions
1. At what times in my life have I experienced the power of the Spirit working through me?
2. In what ways have I carried out the role of being a midwife? Who were the people that were involved?
3. Has anyone been a midwife to me? What were the circumstances?

Guidelines for large-group presentations

Retreats use a variety of large-group presentations. These include the initial welcome and introduction to the retreat, prayer services, icebreakers, a reconciliation service, the introduction to liturgy preparation, the introduction to a film, the wrap-up, and even announcements.

The following are guidelines for training staff to give presentations to large groups:

1. Focus on the purpose of the presentation, the length of time allowed for it, and the different ways the material might be presented.

2. Prepare an outline of the presentation—an outline that includes an introduction, the core

message of the presentation, personal examples, and a summary. Later, the outline can be transferred to index cards that can be used for delivering the presentation.

3. Write out the talk according to the prepared outline. The following are suggestions for writing the presentation:

- **Have a clear message.** After the presentation, the retreatants should be able to repeat the main message. Do not confuse them with a lot of ideas. Focus on one idea in particular.
- **Speak in the first person.** Speak as one person to another person, sharing what is in your heart. Do not speak as an expert or as an adult speaking to a young person.
- **Avoid moralizing.** "You should . . ." messages are usually tuned out by young people. Choose words like "I strongly encourage you . . ." or "I challenge you . . ." or "I hope you will seriously consider. . . ." These words leave the decision up to the individual. Using *should* implies that you know what is good for someone else, and most of the time you really do not.
- **Give directions twice.** This is particularly helpful when you are explaining procedures such as icebreakers or assigning times and places.
- **Use personal examples.** Young people connect with real-life experiences.

4. Record your presentation and listen to it with another person before delivering it. A discussion of the taped presentation can help the presenter to clarify the message and improve the delivery.

5. Test voice volume before delivering the presentation during the retreat. Have a second person check the volume from the back of the room. Also at this time take a few minutes, either privately or with the team, to pray that God will inspire the words spoken and that God will touch and open the hearts of the retreatants.

6. Be conscious of making eye contact with the retreatants. Making eye contact helps to maintain the attention of the listeners and also keeps them aware that you know what else might be going on in the room. If there are disturbances, do not ignore them, but at the same time try not to overreact.

Training for small-group facilitation

A format that works well in training staff members for facilitating small-group discussions is to have them experience a small-group discussion firsthand. The following steps can help you, as the trainer, to lead the staff in such a discussion:

1. Decide on a topic for the small-group discussion. Use one of the topics that will be used during the retreat itself.

2. Gather the retreat team and, using the directions for leading small groups included in one of the retreats (see, for example, the small-group discussion on Christian service on page 40), facilitate the discussion. Alert the staff to note feelings, concerns, and insights experienced during the group discussion. This sensitizes them to feelings, concerns, and insights the retreatants might experience during their small-group discussions.

3. After the group discussion is completed, invite the group to talk about feelings, concerns, and insights that arose during the discussion. Drawing upon their experience of the discussion, identify specific techniques that might be helpful in facilitating a small-group discussion during the retreat. For example, ask:
- What would have helped you feel more at ease?
- What would have helped you to participate more fully in the discussion?

If the training discussion involves the sharing of religious beliefs, there will be the added advantage of the staff members having articulated these beliefs before the retreat, enabling them to better share with the retreatants during the retreat.

4. Have the small-group facilitators list on an index card the purposes of the small-group discussion they are to facilitate and to make a list of tasks and techniques to be used to achieve those purposes. Other announcements or directions that need to be given can be added to this card.

5. The following are suggestions for facilitating discussions:
- Address the retreatants by their first name.
- Protect the retreatants from being pressured to reveal more personal information than they are comfortable in doing.
- Before jumping right into discussion, it is good to give everyone an opportunity to reflect on the questions provided in the retreat descriptions and their responses to them, even to jot down a few things. This will make it easier for shy or less verbal people to respond.

- Re-direct discussion that sidetracks the group from the topic of the discussion.
- Remind the retreatants of the small-group discussion guidelines whenever necessary. (Developing these guidelines will be a task of the retreatants during the retreat.) Make sure the guidelines include confidentiality, respect, no put-downs, honesty, and an attempt to participate by all.
- Use personal examples to make a point.
- Stress the importance of confidentiality.
- Avoid moralizing.
- If the retreatants have difficulty beginning the discussion because they are nervous, pair two people together. Pairing is also a good technique when time is limited.
- Arrange the chairs or the pillows so the retreatants are in a circle or a semicircle. This helps the retreatants to have eye contact with one another.
- Take a few minutes to center yourself before you begin, and pray that God will help you to be sensitive to the needs of the retreatants and that God will touch and open the hearts of the retreatants.

Guidelines for choosing and training young staff members

There are good reasons for using adolescents on the retreat staff team. The experience in ministry is good for the young people on the team. In some situations, peer ministers can be more effective than adults. And at times you may not be able to find enough adults to staff the retreat team.

When you have young people on the retreat team, remember the three areas in which developmental growth is taking place: psychologically, they are trying to establish identity; physically, hormonal changes are influencing a variety of behaviors; spiritually, they are clarifying personal religious beliefs. Affirm their experience, help them articulate their beliefs, and encourage them to continue to grow in their relationship with God and others.

Consider the following guidelines as ways to support young staff members:

- **Select competent candidates.** In choosing young staff members, look for genuineness, empathy, a capacity for self-discipline, listening skills, and the ability to learn from training. Also look for young people who already have a good balance of relationships with peers and adults.

- **Provide preretreat training.** When you are preparing young people to give large-group presentations or to facilitate small-group discussions, you can use the same guidelines used for training the adults. You might even train them along with the adults. It would be mutually beneficial to adolescent and adult team members to practice scenarios rehearsing how the adolescent staff member will act in stressful situations, for instance, handling a disturbance during a large-group presentation or an outburst of emotion during a small-group discussion.

    Likewise, a consideration of the ministerial roles by adults and adolescent staff members together would be mutually helpful. Discuss what to do if, for example, a retreatant confides that she is considering an abortion, a retreatant talks about being physically abused at home, a retreatant blames God for the death of her or his mother, a retreatant is using drugs, and so on.

- **Provide in-service training.** In-service training during the retreat will be especially valuable and reassuring to the young staff member. Ensuring the opportunity and time for discussing problems that emerge during the retreat may be the most important strategy for helping young staff members to know how to respond in stressful situations. Be careful not to overreact or jump into the situation too visibly. It is important that an adult not rush in as a savior.

- **Provide needed follow-up.** Follow-up may be necessary for some young staff members. A young person on a retreat team will be placed in a new relationship with his or her peers. For instance, a retreatant might use drugs in the presence of the adolescent staff member. The adolescent staff member then will have to act in an authority role. The behavior must be named and brought to the attention of an adult. A resulting split between the young staff member and the peers can have lasting effects. If something like this happens, you may have to provide follow-up support that helps the young staff member move back to his or her peers on a more normative basis.

Having young people on the retreat team can be enjoyable and effective. Just be sure to *prepare* and *support* them properly.

Questionnaire for Retreat Staff Candidates

Name _____ Date of birth _____

Address _____

City _____ State _____ Zip _____

Home phone _____ Work phone _____

In order to assist the retreat director in choosing a retreat team, please supply the following information.

Dates you are available:

_____

_____

If you are a student, list your current grade level and the school you attend.

_____

Retreat Experience
▶ Give a brief description of your retreat experience. Include the types of retreats (for example, overnight, day, spiritual-direction, silent) and your role during the retreats (for example, staff member, observer, retreatant).

_____

_____

_____

_____

_____

Religious Education
▶ List religious education courses and other enrichment programs you have attended.

_____

_____

_____

_____

_____

Handout 3–A: Permission to reproduce this handout is granted.

Questionnaire for Retreat Staff Candidates ▽ 2

Personal

▶ List how you would like to help on the retreat (priest, musician, recreation supervisor, small-group facilitator, large-group speaker, prayer-service leader, and so on.) _____

_____

▶ List some of your talents (for example, musician, athlete, audiovisual equipment operator, artist, comedian, good listener, driver, organizer, typist, facilitator, singer, cook) _____

_____

▶ List some of your other interests or hobbies (for example, classical music, biking, surfing, camping, hiking) _____

_____

Ratings

▶ Please rate yourself on your ability and comfort level in the following areas (1=poor, 2=fair, 3=very good, 4=expert)

	ability	comfort level
small-group facilitator	____	____
large-group speaker	____	____
recreation leader	____	____
icebreaker leader	____	____
prayer-service leader	____	____
counseling psychological issues	____	____
education in church-related issues	____	____
spiritual director	____	____
flexibility	____	____
respectfully enforcing rules	____	____
getting along with other staff	____	____
getting along with young people	____	____

Staff Member Medical-Release Form

Name _____

Date of birth _____

Address _____

City _____ State _____ Zip _____

Home phone _____ Work phone _____

In the event of an emergency when medical treatment is required, I give permission to the retreat director to obtain the services of a licensed physician.

Please be aware of the following medical conditions for me:

_____

_____

_____

In the event of an emergency, please notify the following person:

Name _____ Relationship _____

Address _____

City _____ State _____ Zip _____

Home phone _____ Work phone _____

Family Physician

Name _____ Phone _____

Address _____

City _____ State _____ Zip _____

Signature _____
                                (staff member)

Date _____

Reflections on Ministerial Roles

Christian-Adult Role Model

"Let us love in deed and in truth and not merely talk about it" (1 John 3:18).

1. How might I best model Jesus' way for the retreatants?
2. What kind of situations might be the greatest challenge to my being a Christian-adult role model for the retreatants?
3. Who have been Christian-adult role models for me?

Faith Witness

"The Spirit God has given us is no cowardly spirit, but rather one that makes us strong, loving, and wise. Therefore, never be ashamed of your testimony to our Lord" (2 Timothy 1:7–8).

1. How have I been a faith witness to others?
2. Have there been times when prayer has helped me in being a faith witness to others?
3. In what ways do I see myself being a faith witness to the retreatants?

Educator

"Now then, teacher of others, are you failing to teach yourself?" (Romans 2:21).

1. In what ways do I see myself carrying out the role of being an educator for the retreatants?
2. In what areas do I need some additional knowledge for carrying out the role of educator during the retreat?
3. How can I best translate into adolescent language the meanings of church belief and teachings for young people while remaining faithful to their truth?

Counselor

"Love is patient. . . . Love . . . is not self-seeking" (1 Corinthians 13:4–5).

1. What skills and experience do I have that will help me carry out the role of counselor during the retreat?
2. What kinds of counseling situations would I need to refer to an appropriate agency?
3. What are signs to me that new growth is taking place in another person?

Midwife

"If anyone is in Christ, he is a new creation. The old order has passed away; now all is new!" (2 Corinthians 5:17).

1. At what times in my life have I experienced the power of the Spirit working through me?
2. In what ways have I carried out the role of being a midwife? Who were the people that were involved?
3. Has anyone been a midwife to me? What were the circumstances?

Part B ▽

One-Day Retreats

Part B contains three one-day retreats.

Chapter 4, "Come, Let Us Return to the Lord," is designed to be attended by pairs that consist of a teenage retreatant and a parent. A pair can be a daughter-mother, daughter-father, son-mother, or son-father combination. Each parent-teen couple has the opportunity to spend prayerful and playful times together as well as prepare for the season of Lent.

Chapter 5, "We Are Christ's Hands," is intended for eleventh- and twelfth-grade retreatants. The program provides young people with an opportunity to reflect on the call to follow Jesus by giving our time and talents in service to others.

Chapter 6, "Lean on Me," is a graduation retreat for eighth graders. The retreatants are asked to reflect on grade school memories, examine hopes for the future, and celebrate their friendship with Jesus and with one another.

4

Come, Let Us Return to the Lord: A Parent-Teen Lenten Retreat

"Come, Let Us Return to the Lord" is a one-day Lenten retreat designed for ten to twenty-five parent-teen couples. The parent and the teen have the opportunity to enjoy each other's company as well as to deepen their relationship with each other and with the Lord during the season of Lent.

Lent is a time for persons already joined to Jesus in their Baptism to return to the Lord in a new and deeper relationship. Young people ordinarily do not connect Lent with a deepening of relationships. More often, they see Lent as a time when they are not to do certain things that they like, such as watch television or eat desserts. This retreat takes a positive approach to Lent. It provides opportunities for the young person and the parent to share in ways that deepen their relationship with each other and with Jesus and, in doing so, prepare them for the Easter celebration.

Goals

The goals of this retreat are the following:
- That the retreatants examine their understanding about and approach to the season of Lent
- That the retreatants reflect on their relationship with Jesus through dialog, the Scriptures, and prayer
- That the retreat couples discuss ways that they might deepen their relationship with each other and with the Lord during Lent

Schedule

9:30 a.m.	Arrival
10:00 a.m.	Introduction and prayer
10:45 a.m.	Small groups: Introductions and goal setting
11:45 a.m.	Quiet time
12:15 p.m.	Lunch
1:00 p.m.	Recreation
2:00 p.m.	Parent-teen dialog
3:15 p.m.	Break
3:45 p.m.	Roundup
4:00 p.m.	Liturgy
4:45 p.m.	Wrap-up
5:00 p.m.	Departure

Materials needed for this retreat: blank name tags, copies of handouts, a list of the members of each small group, printed stations of the cross for distribution, lunch and soft drinks, snacks for the afternoon break, a Bible for each person, and writing materials (See also the section "Materials Generally Needed for a Retreat" on page 16 of this manual.)

Retreat Activities

9:30 a.m. Arrival

Two staff members welcome and register the retreatants and have them fill out name tags.

10:00 a.m. Introduction and prayer

The introduction is a time to welcome the retreatants and to help them feel more comfortable as they begin the retreat. Most of the retreatants will be a bit apprehensive because they do not know what to expect. Explaining the schedule and inviting questions during this time helps make the retreatants more comfortable.

Staff: two people (the retreat leader and one person to assist with the handouts). All staff members need to be present for introductions.

Materials needed: handout 4–A and a list of the members of each small group

Description of activities

1. Introduction: Say something like the following to introduce the theme of the retreat: "Lent is a time to prepare ourselves for celebrating the joy of Easter. The Church saves 'alleluia' responses, white vestments, and white altar cloths for the Resurrection celebration. During Lent, we wait and prepare to celebrate the Resurrection of Jesus in a new and deeper way.

"This waiting and preparatory season can truly be a time of conversion. By 'conversion' I mean returning, in a new way, to Jesus, whom we were joined to in our Baptism.

"Returning to the Lord is never only an individual affair. The sixth chapter of Matthew's Gospel connects Lenten practices like prayer, fasting, and giving to needy people with the deepening of relationships. Prayer nurtures and deepens our relationship with God. Fasting is a means of self-discipline that increases the self-control and compassion needed in building good relationships. Giving to needy people is a way of giving in relationships with others, especially during times of need. So returning to the Lord during Lent includes renewal and deepening of relationships with others, especially those who are intimately a part of our life.

"The theme that we have chosen for this Lenten retreat fits well with the season of Lent. It is 'Come, Let Us Return to the Lord.' In the Book of Joel, God says, 'Return to me with your whole heart' [2:12]. Let us make this retreat a major part of our returning to the Lord in the newest and most holy way possible, especially by having deepened our relationships with those who are intimately a part of our life.

"During this day you will have the opportunity to reflect upon your relationship with Jesus through the Scriptures and prayer, to deepen your relationship with your partner through dialog, and to discuss with your partner practices that you might adopt during the season of Lent."

2. Opening prayer: Lead the retreat community in prayer, using handout 4–A, "Scriptural Prayer: Psalm 86."

3. Orientation: Explain the guidelines for using the facility and introduce the staff.

4. Grouping: Divide the retreatants into small groups. Place parents together in peer groups, balancing the number of men and women whenever possible. Also place the young people together in peer groups. Separate them by age so that older teens are grouped together and younger teens are grouped together. (A list of these groups should be prepared ahead of time.)

Direct the groups to the sites for their small-group activity.

10:45 a.m. Small groups: Introductions and goal setting

Adults and young people may have different experiences of Lent. Many adults were raised before the changes from Vatican Council II were implemented. Most adults will welcome the opportunity to talk about their experiences with and feelings toward these changes. On the other hand, many young people will have a difficult time talking about their experience of Lent. For some of them, it may have no meaning. For this reason, experienced facilitators of discussions with young people should lead their small groups.

This small-group discussion gives the retreatants time to reflect on their relationship with their retreat partner as well as on their approach to Lent. Vocalizing their feelings and hearing others do the same can give the retreatants a new perspective. The discussion facilitators give the retreatants an opportunity in a peer-support setting to (*a*) describe their relationship with their partner, (*b*) discuss their understanding and experience of Lent, and (*c*) set goals for Lent and for the retreat.

Staff: one person for each small group

Materials needed: paper and pencils

Description of activities

1. Introductions: Invite the group members to introduce themselves, name their retreat partner, and relate their hopes or expectations for the day.

2. Discussion: Distribute paper and pencils. The discussion is divided into two parts. Part b is not to be answered until all group members have answered part a.

a. Have each person write down and share with the group three words that describe his or her retreat partner and then elaborate on any one of those three words. (This response will be used during the roundup activity at 3:45 p.m.)

b. Have each person recall a Lenten practice that he or she has previously done and give a reason for doing it.

3. Goal setting: After all members of the group have reflected upon their feelings about their partner and their previous approaches to Lent, they are in a good position to formulate new personal goals for Lent and for this retreat. Formulating goals for themselves will move them in self-set directions.

a. Have each person name a personal goal for Lent. Suggest that if possible this goal should include their partner in some way.

b. Have each person name a goal for this retreat. Again, suggest that if possible this goal should include their partner in some way.

4. Summary: Summarize the discussion for the group and invite the members to make closing comments that include any new insights about their partner or about the meaning of Lent.

11:45 a.m. Quiet time

Staff: one person to explain the activity and distribute handouts

Materials needed: handout 4–B, Bibles, printed stations of the cross, pencils and paper

Description of activities: Explain to the retreatants that this scheduled quiet time allows them to reflect on their relationship with Jesus—especially in terms of the goals they have set for Lent and for this retreat, ways to carry them out, and their relationship with their partner. They might also consider celebrating the Sacrament of Penance if a priest is available. Pass out handout 4–B, "Reflection Questions for Quiet Time."

Retreatants may spend this time walking, journal writing, making the stations of the cross, or reading the Passion (Matthew, chapters 26—27; Mark, chapters 14—15; Luke, chapters 22—23; John, chapters 18—19).

Younger retreatants may find it difficult to spend this time alone. Encourage walking while reflecting. This might be easier than sitting still for the entire scheduled time.

12:15 p.m. Lunch

One staff person should be available to make announcements and to choose a retreatant to lead the group in prayer before the meal.

1:00 p.m. Recreation

Encourage the retreatants to recreate with their partner. Team games, like volleyball or relays, might be suggested for the active, and icebreakers (found in several of the other retreat programs in this manual) might work well with the less active.

2:00 p.m. Parent-teen dialog

This activity can help the parent-teen relationship by providing the opportunity for partners to communicate on a meaningful and personal level. In introducing this activity, stress the importance of personal sharing for deepening relationships.

Staff: two people (one to assist with distributing handouts and helping retreatants relocate for the dialog)

Materials needed: pencils and handout 4–C

Description of activities

1. Introduction: Discuss the importance of sharing on a personal level for the deepening of relationships. Use words like the following: "Any healthy relationship has been helped along by taking time to honestly communicate thoughts and feelings. During the typical day, all of us are kept busy as students, employees, homemakers, and so on. We have little time to engage in conversation about things that are personally important.

"By coming to this retreat, you have taken time to build your relationship with God and with your partner. Until now, your contact with your partner during this retreat has been unstructured. But this activity involves a process for speaking and listening to your partner. The topic will be your understanding of and approach to the season of Lent. In your speaking and listening to one another, you will be strengthening your communication skills and your relationship with each other.

"You will receive a list of questions to assist you in your dialog. Use them as a guide. Feel free to go beyond them in your conversation. Remember, this is your time together as parent and daughter or son."

2. Explanation of the activity: "You will have ten minutes for quiet reflection on the questions. After the ten minutes, join your partner and go to a place by yourselves for a structured communication exercise.

"During your first ten minutes together, the parent will speak to the young person. All the young person needs to do is listen. Next, for ten minutes the young person, using the same guide questions, will speak while the parent listens. In the following twenty minutes you may share freely without any guiding questions. An announcement will be made for changing from one activity to the next. After the unstructured twenty-minute period, we will gather again as a large group."

Distribute handout 4-C, "Parent-Teen Dialog Questions," along with pencils.

3. Time changes: Announce the times for changing from one activity to the next.
- ten minutes: private, quiet reflection on questions
- ten minutes: parent speaks to young person; young person listens
- ten minutes: young person speaks to parent; parent listens
- twenty minutes: young person and parent speak freely

4. Closure: Invite all of the retreatants to return to their original seat. Encourage them to comment on the experience.

3:15 p.m. Break

During the break, have a staff member choose retreatants to help with the liturgy. Be sure to include parents as well as young people. Responsibilities include the following:
- reading the first reading: Ezek. 37:12-14
- reading the response: "The Lord is kind and merciful," with Ps. 103:1-2,3-4,8,10,12-13
- reading the second reading: 2 Tim. 1:8-10
- presenting the offertory gifts
- serving as eucharistic ministers

3:45 p.m. Roundup

In this activity, retreatants have the opportunity to make closing comments. The leader invites each retreatant to respond to a set of questions about the retreat.

Staff: one person to lead the activity. All staff members need to be present.

Materials needed: handout 4-D

Description of activities: Ask the retreatants to sit in a circle. Give them handout 4-D, "Roundup Questions," and time to read the questions. Then, going around the circle, invite each retreatant to respond orally to the questions on the handout. After everyone has had an opportunity to respond to the questions, invite the retreatants to offer any other closing comments. Those who were initially hesitant to respond usually use this opportunity to participate.

4:00 p.m. Liturgy

Retreatants carry out those parts of the liturgy for which they are responsible. An appropriate gospel reading would be John 11:1-45.

4:45 p.m. Wrap-up

Staff: one person (the same person who led the introduction and prayer in the morning)

Materials needed: none

Description of activities

1. Closing presentation: "Today has been special. You and your partner have taken the time during this Lent to deepen your relationship with each other and with Jesus by sharing in personal ways. You have talked together, played together, eaten together, and celebrated a liturgy together. We hope that in doing these things, you have turned to each other in a new way and have returned to the Lord together.

"Now you have the challenge to return to your home, school, and workplace and keep alive the new growth that has taken place within you. Take steps on a regular basis to nourish your deepened relationship with each other and with the Lord. In a few weeks, at Easter, we will celebrate the love that the Risen Jesus continues to pour out to us. My prayer for you is that your Lenten practices will draw you ever closer to each other, to other people, and especially to the Lord Jesus."

2. Announcements

5:00 p.m. Departure

Scriptural Prayer: Psalm 86

Right: Teach me your way, Yahweh,
and I will obey you faithfully;
give me an undivided heart
that I may fear your name.

Left: I will praise you with all my heart, O my God;
I will proclaim your greatness forever.

Right: Great is your faithful love for me!
You have saved me from the depths of the grave.

Left: Yahweh, you are a compassionate and loving God,
slow to anger, always kind and faithful.

All: Teach me your way, Yahweh,
and I will obey you faithfully;
give me an undivided heart
that I may fear your name.

(Psalm 86:11–13,15)

Reflection Questions for Quiet Time

Directions: The following questions are provided to help you reflect during this quiet time. You might also consider the suggestions given below.

1. How does the goal I have set for this retreat strengthen my relationship with my partner? with Jesus?

2. What do I need to do today to accomplish my retreat goal?

3. How does the goal I have set for Lent strengthen my relationship with Jesus? with my partner?

4. Do any of my relationships with other people need to be renewed or strengthened during this Lenten time?

5. How would celebrating the Sacrament of Penance help me in strengthening my relationship with Jesus? with my partner? with other people?

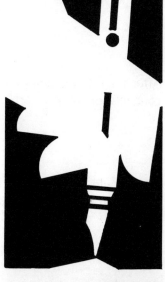

Suggestions for Enriching Reflection

▶ walking
▶ journal writing
▶ making the stations of the cross
▶ reading the Passion:
   Matthew, chapters 26–27
   Mark, chapters 14–15
   Luke, chapters 22–23
   John, chapters 18–19

Handout 4–B: Permission to reproduce this handout is granted.

Parent-Teen Dialog Questions

Directions: You will be given ten minutes for individual reflection and writing, using the questions below for a guide. After ten minutes, join your partner and go to a place by yourselves for a structured communication exercise. During the first ten minutes, the parent will speak to the young person. Next, for ten minutes the young person will speak. Then for twenty minutes you may share freely without any guiding questions.

1. What does Lent mean to you?

2. What would you, individually, like to do for Lent?

3. What is your goal for this retreat?

4. After the retreat, what can you and your partner do together to grow in your relationship?

5. What could you and your partner and your whole family do together to strengthen family relationships during Lent?

6. What are ways that you might individually deepen your relationship with with Jesus during Lent?

7. What could you and your whole family do together to deepen your family's relationship with Jesus during Lent?

Handout 4–C: Permission to reproduce this handout is granted.

Retreat Roundup Questions

Directions: Read and reflect on the following questions for discussion.

1. What three words did you use this morning to describe your retreat partner?

   ▶ After spending the day with your partner, what new words would you use to describe him or her?

2. What was your goal for this retreat?

   ▶ Did you accomplish this goal?

   ▶ What helped or hindered you in this regard?

3. What Lenten resolutions have you made today that you would like to share with the whole group?

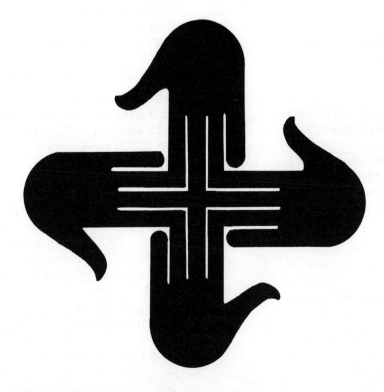

Handout 4–D: Permission to reproduce this handout is granted.

5

We Are Christ's Hands: A Discipleship Retreat

"We Are Christ's Hands" is a one-day retreat designed for twenty to forty eleventh and twelfth graders.

When Pope John Paul II came to the United States in September 1987, he chose for the theme of his visit "Unity in the Work of Service." The pope urged us to consider ways that we, the followers of Jesus, can serve the world through selfless deeds. He reminded us that followers of Jesus Christ grow in unity as they render service to others.

This retreat challenges the retreatants to grow in a commitment of service to others. Young people do become less self-centered and begin to look at the needs of others as they mature. But they need challenges and encouragement to move this new perspective into action.

Goals

The goals of this retreat are the following:
- That the retreatants examine their personal call to Christian service
- That the retreatants examine the importance of prayer in a life of Christian service
- That the retreatants consider specific ways to render service to others in the name of Jesus Christ

Schedule

9:00 a.m. Arrival
9:30 a.m. Introduction and prayer
10:15 a.m. Input 1: Presentation on Christian service
10:45 a.m. Quiet time
11:00 a.m. Small group 1: Christian service discussion
12:15 p.m. Lunch
1:00 p.m. Recreation
2:15 p.m. Input 2: Presentation on prayer and Christian service
2:45 p.m. Quiet time
3:15 p.m. Small group 2: Prayer and Christian service
4:30 p.m. Break
5:00 p.m. Liturgy
5:45 p.m. Wrap-up
6:00 p.m. Departure

Optional schedule to fit within a school day

8:30 a.m. Arrival
9:00 a.m. Introduction and prayer
9:45 a.m. Input 1: A presentation on Christian service
10:15 a.m. Quiet time
10:30 a.m. Small group 1: Christian service discussion
11:30 a.m. Lunch and recreation
12:45 p.m. Input 2: A presentation on prayer and Christian service
1:15 p.m. Quiet time
1:45 p.m. Small group 2: Prayer and Christian service
2:30 p.m. Break
2:45 p.m. Liturgy
3:30 p.m. Wrap-up
3:45 p.m. Departure

Materials needed for this retreat: blank name tags; lunch and soft drinks; a Bible for each retreatant; writing materials; the song "Saint Theresa's Prayer"; a record or tape player; the book *Words to Love By . . . ,* by Mother Teresa; copies of handouts; felt-tip markers; butcher paper; masking tape; and a notebook for each retreatant, to be used for journal writing (See also the section "Materials Generally Needed for a Retreat" on page 16 of this manual.)

Retreat Activities

9:00 a.m. Arrival

Two staff members welcome and register the retreatants and have them fill out name tags.

9:30 a.m. Introduction and prayer

The introduction is a time to welcome the retreatants and to help them prepare for the day. Because this activity sets the tone for the day, it is important that the leader speak directly to the issue of Christian service and truly challenge the retreatants to see beyond what they have previously envisioned as Christian service.

Staff: two people (the retreat leader and one person to assist with the handouts). All staff members need to be present for introductions.

Materials needed: a Bible; the song "Saint Theresa's Prayer" from the album *Heart of the Shepherd,* by John Michael Talbot; and a record or tape player

Description of activities

1. Introduction: Introduce the theme of the retreat by saying something like the following: "In Saint John's Gospel [15:9–17], Jesus tells his followers, 'Live on in my love.' He then commands, 'Love one another as I have loved you.' This is the command that Jesus still gives to all of his followers today. When we choose to call ourselves Christians, we have a responsibility to try to follow the teachings of Jesus.

"Our Church reminds us to listen to the words of Jesus. When Pope John Paul II came to the United States in September 1987, he chose for the theme of his visit 'Unity in the Work of Service.' At that time, the pope urged us to consider ways that we, the followers of Jesus, can serve the world through selfless deeds.

"Vatican Council II stated that the role of the Church, or the people of God, is to 'spread the kingdom of Christ' ["Decree on the Apostolate of Lay People," no. 2]. We are the hands of Christ to others. People see the love of Christ through our loving actions.

" 'We Are Christ's Hands' is the name of this retreat. Throughout the day you will be encouraged to examine ways that you can be Christ's hands in service to others—a topic that some people find difficult to accept. This retreat will be a challenge to you. You will be urged to go beyond a comfortable lifestyle."

2. Retreat goals: Encourage the retreatants to set a personal goal for the day. Allow for some quiet time at this point so the retreatants can set their goal.

3. Prayer: "Lord Jesus, you have come to show us how to live our life in service to others. You command us to love one another as you love us. We desire to follow your commands, yet we often stumble because it is easier to let others love us and not give of ourselves. During our day of retreat, we pray that you will help us find ways to follow you more closely. Most importantly, though, we pray that upon leaving this retreat, we will remember our call as your followers to bring your love to others, to be your hands to the world. We offer our prayer in your name as Jesus, our Teacher and Friend."

End the opening prayer by playing the song "Saint Theresa's Prayer" from the album *Heart of the Shepherd,* by John Michael Talbot, as a quiet meditation.

4. Orientation: Explain the guidelines for using the retreat facility and introduce the staff. If the retreatants come from a variety of places, consider having them introduce themselves to one another at this time. Or perhaps use one of the icebreakers found elsewhere in this manual.

10:15 a.m. Input 1: Presentation on Christian service

The leader of this activity introduces the retreatants to the importance of Christian service. This topic can be unsettling for people who are uncomfortable with giving time and energy in service to others. The presenter must challenge the retreatants during this talk. Using personal examples can help them see that this call to service is for all Christians, not only for priests or brothers and sisters, who are expected to make helping others their life work.

Staff: one person

Materials needed: a copy of the book *Words to Love By...*, by Mother Teresa

Description of activities

1. Introduction: "In her book *Words to Love By...* [Notre Dame, IN: Ave Maria Press, 1983], Mother Teresa states that if we preoccupy ourselves with talking *about* poor people, we don't have time to talk *to* poor people [p. 25]. In other words, we must put our words into action. Always talking about service to others does not allow us enough time to be of service to others."

2. Presentation: Tell the retreatants your own story of service to others, using the following outline as a guide:

a. Name some of the people who have influenced your growth in the Christian commitment of service to others (e.g., parents, teachers, Dr. Martin Luther King, Jr., Mother Teresa, Elizabeth Ann Seton) and explain how they influenced you.
b. Describe some comfortable and uncomfortable feelings that you have experienced while helping others (e.g., peace, sadness, confusion).
c. Explain what Christian service means to you and why it is a value to you.

Your honesty will be an invitation for the retreatants to examine their own story. Keep your statements simple and clear.

3. Conclusion: Summarize your presentation.

10:45 a.m. Quiet time

Staff: two people (including one to assist in the distribution of handouts, pencils, and journals)

Materials needed: handout 5–A, pencils, and journals

Description of activities: Pass out handout 5–A, "Christian Service." Explain that the retreatants should reflect quietly on the handout questions. Encourage them to write their reflections in their journal.

Assign the retreatants to groups of seven or eight people and state where the groups will be meeting later. After the quiet time, ask the retreatants to go directly to the small-group meeting places.

11:00 a.m. Small group 1: Christian service discussion

This discussion on Christian service may initially be difficult for the retreatants. As the trust level increases, however, the retreatants may feel more comfortable sharing their thoughts and feelings. Group leaders can help the retreatants by being patient and encouraging all of them to participate to some degree. This activity is meant only to plant the seed for Christian service. Do not try to force immediate outcomes. Growth in Christian commitment comes after prayer, time, and hearing the call of Jesus. (A review of the training for small-group facilitation on page 23 of this manual might be helpful to staff members preparing for this activity.)

Staff: one person for each small group

Materials needed: handout 5–A, a felt-tip marker, butcher paper, and masking tape

Description of activities

1. Introductions: Invite each retreatant to introduce herself or himself to the group.

2. Guidelines: Ask the retreatants to describe a good discussion. Using that description, help them formulate guidelines that will help in their discussion (see page 41). Post these guidelines for all to see.

3. Discussion: List the following questions on a piece of butcher paper and hang the list for all to see. Pair the retreatants and have them ask each other the questions. (Be sure the retreatants have retained handout 5–A from the previous activity.)
- What was your reaction to the earlier presentation on Christian service?
- Which question on the handout was the most difficult for you to answer?
- Which question on the handout was the easiest for you to answer?

Next, offer the opportunity for group members to respond to the whole group about any of the questions on the handout.

4. Closure: Summarize the group's discussion. Invite everyone to make a closing comment. Invite a retreatant from the group to offer a closing prayer.

12:15 p.m. Lunch

One staff person should be available to make announcements and to choose a retreatant to lead the group in prayer before the meal.

1:00 p.m. Recreation

This recreational period is to be unstructured, but have recreational equipment available. Weather permitting, encourage the retreatants to go outside for some type of exercise.

2:15 p.m. Input 2:
Presentation on prayer and Christian service

The leader of this activity introduces the retreatants to the importance of prayer in a life of Christian service. This is a personal topic. The willingness of the presenter to share personal experiences will encourage the retreatants to honestly examine their own prayer.

Staff: one person

Materials needed: none

Description of activities

1. Introduction: "This morning we discussed the Christian call to service. Many times we are reluctant to assist when someone needs help. As followers of Jesus, we need to change this feeling of reluctance toward helping others. Part of the answer is prayer. We can ask God to help us become more compassionate, to help us overcome any fears that keep us from being the hands of Jesus for others, and to sustain us when serving others is hard."

2. Presentation: Tell the retreatants your own story of Christian service, using the following outline as a guide:
a. Describe the experiences that taught you to pray about your feelings toward people in need.
b. Explain how prayer has changed your feelings about people in need.
c. Describe how prayer has sustained you during the hard times of Christian service.
d. Name the kinds of prayer that have been effective for you (e.g., prayer groups, praying with the Scriptures, meditation).
e. Explain how prayer and service have made a difference in your life.

3. Summary: Summarize your presentation.

2:45 p.m. Quiet time

Staff: two people (including one to assist with the distribution of handouts)

Materials needed: handout 5-B, Bibles, journals, and pencils

Description of activities: Pass out handout 5-B, "Prayer and Christian Service," asking the retreatants to retain this handout for the following activity. Explain that during this time the retreatants are to reflect quietly on the handout questions. Encourage them to write their reflections in their journal. After the quiet time, ask the retreatants to go directly to the small-group meeting areas they were assigned to earlier.

3:15 p.m. Small group 2:
Prayer and Christian service

During this small-group discussion, each group leader facilitates a discussion on the importance of prayer in doing Christian service. The trust level will probably have increased since the first small-group meeting, so this discussion will be a bit easier. However, respecting the retreatants' experience of prayer and service is important.

Staff: one person for each small group

Materials needed: handout 5-B, a felt-tip marker, butcher paper, and masking tape

Description of activities

1. Guidelines: Review the guidelines for discussion established during the first small-group meeting. Stress the importance of confidentiality.

2. Discussion: Begin the discussion by asking the following questions of the whole group.
- Which question on the handout was the most difficult for you to answer?
- Which question on the handout was the easiest for you to answer?

Offer the opportunity for all members to answer. Tally their responses on butcher paper.

Invite the group members to respond to any of the questions on the handout.

3. Goal review: Ask the retreatants to recall the personal retreat goal they set at the beginning of the day. Ask them to reflect on how that goal might have changed during the day. Invite them to describe to what extent that goal has been achieved at this point.

4. Summary: Summarize the group's discussion. Invite everyone to make a closing comment.

5. Liturgical preparation: One person should be chosen from each small group to assist with the liturgy. Below is a list of responsibilities and suggested readings:
- reading the first reading: Eph. 4:11–16
- reading the response: "I commit myself to you, O Lord," with Ps. 37:3–4,5–6,18–19,27–28
- presenting the offertory gifts (This task could be assigned to two groups, or two representatives could be chosen from one group.)
- serving as eucharistic ministers

6. Closure: Invite a retreatant from the group to offer a closing prayer.

4:30 p.m. Break

During this break, assigned retreatants should prepare for their liturgical responsibilities.

5:00 p.m. Liturgy

Retreatants carry out those parts of the liturgy for which they are responsible. A suggested communion song is "Saint Theresa's Prayer," from the album *Heart of the Shepherd* by John Michael Talbot. An appropriate gospel reading would be John 13:1–17.

5:45 p.m. Wrap-up

Staff: one person

Materials needed: none

Description of activities
1. Introduction: Read the following:

Dear Jesus,
Help us to spread your fragrance everywhere we go. Flood our souls with your spirit and life.
Penetrate and possess our whole being so utterly
    that our lives may only be a radiance of yours.
Shine through us
and be so in us
that every soul we come in contact with
    may feel your presence in our soul.
Let them look up and see no longer us
but only Jesus.
Stay with us
and then we shall begin to shine as you shine,
so to shine as to be light to others.
The light, O Jesus, will be all from you.
None of it will be ours.
It will be you shining on others through us.
Let us thus praise you in the way you love best
    by shining on those around us.
Let us preach you without preaching
    not by words but by our example
    by the catching force
    the sympathetic influence of what we do
    the evident fullness of the love our hearts
        bear to you
                      Amen.
(Mother Teresa, *Words to Love By...*, p. 47)

2. Closure: "I urge each of you to grow in your Christian commitment. Let others come to know Jesus through your words and actions.

"Let this day be a turning point in your life as you begin to realize that Christ has no hands but your hands. Together, as a community of faith and love, we can bring Jesus to the world.

"I will pray for each of you, and I encourage you to pray for one another."

3. Announcements

6:00 p.m. Departure

Because of the late departure time, consider making provisions for a meal, either on site or on the way back from the retreat if the distance is great.

Christian Service

**Let us love in deed
and in truth
and not merely talk about it.
(1 John 3:18)**

Consider the following questions and jot your reflections in your journal.

1. When was the last time that someone asked you to help them? What were your feelings? How did you respond? What is your normal reaction when you are asked to help?

2. Who are some people who have given of their time and energy to help you?

3. What are specific ways that you can give of yourself to others?

4. What makes it difficult for you to be of service to others?

5. What makes it easier for you to be of service to others?

6. What is the personal retreat goal that you set for yourself during the retreat introduction? Has that goal changed?

7. Read Matthew 25:31–46. Write your reflections in your journal.

Handout 5–A: Permission to reproduce this handout is granted.

Prayer and Christian Service

**When you call me,
when you go to pray to me,
I will listen to you.
(Jeremiah 29:12)**

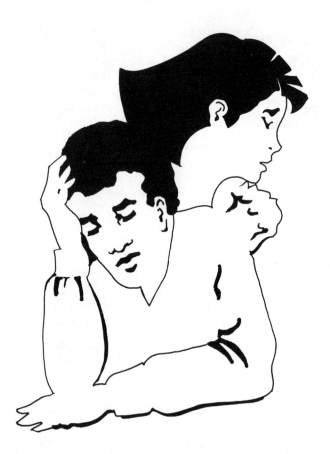

Consider the following questions and jot your reflections in your journal.

1. What is prayer for you?
2. How often do you pray for people in need?
3. How often do you pray for God's help in doing service for others?
4. How do you envision prayer as being helpful in doing service for others?
5. Has this retreat suggested any commitments or resolutions you would like to make for yourself?
6. Read Sirach 2:1–6. Write your reflections in your journal.

6 ▽

Lean on Me: An Eighth-Grade Graduation Retreat

"Lean on Me" is a one-day retreat for eighth graders who are preparing to graduate. The retreat program is designed for twenty to forty participants. This program can be especially effective with a class of eighth graders who have gone to school with one another for a number of years.

The end of the school year is a time of excitement, but it can also be a time of anxiety for the eighth-grade graduate. A transition is about to happen. An ending is about to take place. Good-byes are said to a familiar place where friendships have been formed and achievements made—friendships and achievements that need to be acknowledged and celebrated. At the same time, a new beginning brings new hopes and new fears.

This retreat can help young people through this transition by providing space and time to ask God to bless what has been and to ask God's blessing on what is to come.

Goals

The goals of this retreat are the following:
- That the retreatants share memories of grade school years
- That the retreatants share hopes as they move on to high school
- That the retreatants celebrate friendships, especially the friendship of Jesus

Schedule

9:30 a.m. Arrival
10:00 a.m. Introduction and prayer
10:45 a.m. Icebreakers
11:30 a.m. Small group 1: Memories
12:30 p.m. Lunch with partners
1:00 p.m. Organized recreation
2:00 p.m. Small group 2: Hopes
3:15 p.m. Liturgical preparation
4:15 p.m. Break
4:45 p.m. Liturgy
5:45 p.m. Wrap-up
6:00 p.m. Dinner
7:00 p.m. Departure

Materials needed for this retreat: the song "Lean on Me," a felt-tip marker, butcher paper, masking tape, writing materials, volleyballs and volleyball courts, soft drinks and sack lunches, and food and drink for the closing dinner (See also the section "Materials Generally Needed for a Retreat" on page 16 of this manual.)

Retreat Activities

9:30 a.m. Arrival

Two staff members welcome and register the retreatants.

10:00 a.m. Introduction and prayer

The introduction is a time to welcome the retreatants and to help them feel more comfortable. The eighth-grade retreatants are usually excited and have a lot of nervous energy. Explaining the schedule and inviting any questions during this time helps make the retreatants feel more comfortable.

Staff: two people. All staff members need to be present for introductions.

Materials needed: the song "Lean on Me" from the album *Life, Love, Pain,* by Club Nouveau (If you cannot recruit a retreatant or a staff member who plays an instrument to help lead the song, bring a tape or a record of the song and a tape or record player.)

Description of activities

1. Introduction: Introduce the theme of the retreat with words like the following: "The end of the school year is a busy time for you. You have dances, outings, parties, and final exams, along with your usual responsibilities. During this busy time, it is easy for you to get caught up in the excitement shown to you by your family, teachers, and friends. This is certainly a time to celebrate your academic accomplishments and the friendships you have shared with each other throughout the past eight years.

"There is another friendship I hope you remember to celebrate. That is the friendship you share with Jesus. As you graduate and move on to ninth grade, you start a new beginning in your life. Some of you will have a new school. You will make new friends and meet new teachers and new challenges. This can be exciting as well as a bit frightening. The friendship that you have with Jesus, though, will not be new. You can take his friendship with you wherever you go.

" 'Lean on Me' is the theme for this retreat. Imagine Jesus saying this to you. He invites us daily to let him lighten our burden. When you face difficult times, remember to call on Jesus. Have Jesus with you also when you celebrate good times.

"During the retreat, you will have the chance to talk about your memories of the past eight years as well as your expectations for the future. We share this day together as a Christian community and ask Jesus to be the center of our retreat community."

2. Prayer: "Lord Jesus, we gather in your name today as we begin our retreat. Bless our memories of the past eight years. Walk with us in the future and give us reminders to lean on you. We pray in your name, Lord Jesus, our Friend and Savior."

3. Song: Teach the song "Lean on Me" from the album *Life, Love, Pain,* by Club Nouveau. Many of the retreatants will be familiar with this song. If you have arranged for a retreatant or a staff member who is a musician to lead the song, teach the retreatants the refrain and have the musician sing the verses. If no musician is available, encourage the retreatants to sing along with a recording of the music.

4. Orientation: Explain the guidelines for using the facility and introduce the staff.

10:45 a.m. Icebreakers

The Ducks and Cows icebreaker below not only helps the retreatants feel at ease with one another but also serves to form groups. Groups need to be formed several times in this retreat, so you might want to use the first icebreaker for that purpose.

Staff: one person for each small group. Encourage all staff members to participate.

Materials needed: none

Description of activities

1. Introduction: Explain that the purpose of the icebreakers is to help the retreatants relax and feel more at ease with one another. Give directions for the icebreakers two times. Ask if any retreatants need clarification before you begin the activity.

2. Triangle Tag: Divide the retreatants into groups of four. Three people in each group form a triangle by facing each other and holding hands. The fourth person in each group stands outside the triangle as the chaser. Designate one person in the triangle as the target.

The object of the game is for the chaser to try to tag the target while the three persons forming the triangle try to protect the target by shifting and moving. The target cannot be legally tagged on the hands or arms or from across the triangle.

3. Yurt Circle: Form an even number of retreatants into a circle, facing inward, shoulder to shoulder, and holding hands. Go around the circle and, in alternating fashion, designate persons as *in-persons* and *out-persons,* so that each in-person is in between two out-persons and vice versa.

At the count of three, direct the in-persons to lean toward the center of the circle as far as possible while the out-persons lean back as far as possible. The participants must keep their feet stationary and support one another by holding hands.

Once the yurt circle is stable, have the in-persons and out-persons switch roles while continuing to hold hands. If this works, try switching back and forth in rhythm.

4. Ducks and Cows: Have all the retreatants close their eyes. The leader then whispers the word *duck* or *cow* to each person. (If there is need for more groups, use the names of barnyard creatures that give out a distinct sound, e.g., sheep, rooster.) You might want to instruct the retreatants to keep their hands raised until they have received an identity.

When everyone has been given a barnyard identity, tell them to seek out and group together with the other members of their species by loudly making the sound of the creature they are (for example, quacking, mooing, baaing, or crowing), all the while keeping their eyes closed.

5. Closure: After the icebreakers, ask the retreatants to sit and invite them to share their reactions to the activity. Summarize the activity by reminding the retreatants that the icebreakers were successful because they were working together. Stress that this is true for all retreat activities. Encourage them to bring this attitude to all activities during the retreat. Assign small groups for the next activity. You might wish to use the groups formed during Ducks and Cows.

11:30 a.m. Small group 1: Memories

This group discussion is meant to be an enjoyable experience for the retreatants as they reminisce together. In order to move to the new beginning in a transition, it helps to say good-bye to the past. By sharing memories, the retreatants recall the past and bless the memories. (A review of the training for small-group facilitation on page 23 of this manual might be helpful to staff members preparing to lead this discussion.)

Staff: one person for each small group

Materials needed: a felt-tip marker, butcher paper, masking tape, and writing materials for the retreatants

Description of activities

1. Guidelines: Help the retreatants establish guidelines for discussion and post them for all to see (see page 40).

2. Introductions: Arrange the group in a circle. The retreatants probably know one another, but if not, invite each person to introduce himself or herself to the group.

3. Discussion
a. Go around the circle and ask the retreatants to explain their hopes for the retreat.
b. Distribute pencils and paper to the group members. Lead a discussion about memories in the following manner. Encourage the retreatants to focus on the last eight years. Read aloud the first three questions listed below and ask the retreatants to jot down their answers. Then go around the circle asking each person to share one of her or his responses. Do not pressure anyone to answer. If there is reluctance to respond, simply move on to the next person.

After the entire group has had an opportunity to respond, you can address some or all of the remaining questions to the group as a whole.
- What are your happiest memories?
- What are your funniest memories?
- What are your saddest memories?
- Was there a time when you felt close to God?
- Was there a time when you felt far away from God?
- What accomplishments are you proud of?
- What do you wish you could have done differently?

4. Closure: Summarize the group's discussion. Invite everyone to make a closing comment. Invite a retreatant to offer a closing prayer to bless the memories that have been shared. Explain the schedule for the afternoon.

5. Lunch preparation: Pair each retreatant with the person they know the least in their small group. Begin by asking one person whom they know the least. They will be partners. Continue in this manner until everyone has a partner. If they all say they know one another, pair each retreatant with someone sitting several places distant. Explain to the retreatants that they and their partner will be lunch partners. This means that they will be sitting together for lunch so that they might get to know each other a little better.

There may be some resistance to this. If so, simply explain that they may sit with their friends as a group. However, everyone in the group of friends must be with their partner. (This helps bring the whole group together. By the eighth grade, there are various groups of friends that have developed. By pairing the retreatants, groups that usually would not sit together are brought together for the meal.)

12:30 p.m. Lunch with partners

One staff person should be available to make announcements and to choose a retreatant to lead the grace before the meal.

The retreatants share the meal with the lunch partners assigned during the first small-group meeting.

1:00 p.m. Organized recreation

Staff: two people

Materials needed: two volleyballs and two volleyball courts

Description of activities

1. Divide the retreatants into two or four teams, depending upon the number of retreatants and the number of volleyball courts available. Balance the number of boys and girls on the teams.

2. Explain the rules for Retreat Volleyball. These rules are the same as those for a normal game of volleyball with the following exceptions:
- The ball must be kept moving all of the time.
- Three people on one side of the net must touch the ball before it is hit over the net.
- The ball may bounce once.
- If the ball goes out of the court, it is still in play. The goal is to keep the ball moving, not to score points.

3. Assign the teams to the different courts.

4. Spend about thirty minutes playing volleyball. Announce where and when to meet for the next activity. Allow the retreatants to use the remaining time as they wish.

2:00 p.m. Small group 2: Hopes

This discussion of the retreatants' hopes and expectations for the future will not be as easy as that of small group 1. The retreatants might have some unspoken concerns mixed with the excitement about the transition from eighth grade to high school. Group leaders might find it helpful to begin this discussion by sharing memories of their high school experience. Care should be taken in selecting memories to relate because the retreatants will be listening very intently. Hearing frightening stories will not help them.

Staff: one person for each small group

Materials needed: none

Description of activities

1. Focusing: Direct the retreatants to form into the same groups they were in for the morning small-group discussion. The retreatants have just come from a recreational period, so help them to physically settle down while in their small groups. Give the following directions:

"Sit quietly. Close your eyes. Take a deep breath. Hold it. [Pause three seconds.] Exhale. Do this again. Take a deep breath. Hold it. Exhale.

"Continue to sit quietly with your eyes closed as we prepare to begin our next discussion. As you sit here relaxing, recall the discussion you had this morning about the memories you and your classmates have about the past eight years. Sit quietly with those memories. [Allow about two minutes of silence.]

"Now think about feelings and hopes you have as you prepare for high school. Continue to breathe slowly and relax as you think about these hopes. Soon we will begin a discussion about your hopes for and expectations of the future. [Allow about one minute.]

"Please open your eyes now."

2. Guidelines: Review the discussion guidelines, especially stressing the importance of confidentiality.

3. Discussion: Go around the group and invite each member of the group to share their hopes as they move on to high school. After each member of the group has had an opportunity to respond, address some or all of the following questions to the group as a whole. Allow plenty of time for the retreatants to get in touch with their feelings and thoughts.
- What are your fears as you move on to high school?
- What activities do you wish to join in high school?
- What have you learned from the past that you would like to use in the future?
- What commitments would you like to make for yourself in the areas of family, friends, classes, God, self?
- What will you need to deepen your relationship with Jesus?

Comment on the similarities and differences of their responses. Help the retreatants to explore what in their past has influenced them.

4. Affirmation: Invite the group members to express what they appreciate about each member of the group. Begin by choosing the first person to be affirmed. Encourage all group members to speak directly to that person, saying, "I appreciate _____ about you." Do this affirmation for each person. Do not allow retreatants to speak about past stereotypes they may have had about an individual. Keep them focused on what they appreciate now.

5. Closure: Summarize the group's discussion. Invite everyone to make a closing comment. Invite a retreatant to offer a closing prayer.

3:15 p.m. Liturgical preparation

This is the time when the retreatants can work together as a team. It is a time for them to plan the celebration of their friendships and their friendship with Jesus, with friendship being the theme of the liturgy. Encourage creativity in their preparations.

See the appendix, pages 117–120, for a full explanation of the committees and instructions for presenting this session on liturgical preparation to the retreatants.

4:15 p.m. Break

4:45 p.m. Liturgy

The committees carry out those parts of the liturgy for which they are responsible.

5:45 p.m. Wrap-up

Staff: one person

Materials needed: none

Description of activities: Make any announcements and give a presentation like the following:

"You have spent this day recalling your grade school memories and discussing your hopes for high school. Bless the memories and thank God for the many gifts you have received.

"You have also celebrated your friendships with each other and your friendship with Jesus. Some of your friends will be going to different schools next year. There will be less time for you to spend together.

"Just as you will make efforts to keep your friendships with others alive, I hope you will also take time to keep your friendship with Jesus alive. Take time to pray daily. Lean on him during hard times and remember to celebrate with him during good times.

"We will pray for each of you. I encourage you to do the same for one another."

6:00 p.m. Dinner

This meal is designed to be a continuation of the celebration of friendships. Allow adequate time for the retreatants to enjoy the time with one another.

A suggested menu is hot dogs or hamburgers with chips or potato salad. Some people like to prepare lasagna or casseroles because they are easy to make for large groups. My experience with young people has been that they do not like casseroles because they are uncertain of the ingredients!

One staff person should be available to make announcements and to choose a retreatant to lead the grace before the meal.

7:00 p.m. Departure

Part C ▽

Two-Day Retreats

Part C contains two overnight retreats.

Chapter 7, "Prepare the Way of the Lord," is an Advent retreat designed for eighth, ninth, and tenth graders. It provides the retreatants with the opportunity to prepare for the birth of Jesus.

Chapter 8, "Change My Heart, O God," is directed at alcohol and drug abuse. It can be used with any age-group of teenagers. This retreat will be beneficial for people who have never misused alcohol or drugs as well as for people who are currently struggling with an abuse problem.

7 ▽

Prepare the Way of the Lord: An Advent Retreat

"Prepare the Way of the Lord" is an overnight retreat designed to accommodate twenty to forty eighth, ninth, and tenth graders.

Advent is a liturgical season accompanied by joy and hopeful expectations. So much takes place at this time in the way of family gatherings, family travel, Christmas preparations, final exams, ski trips, and so on that it is easy to lose the meaning of Advent. This retreat provides the time and space for the retreatants to step aside from the busyness of these days to prepare themselves for a new birth of Jesus in their heart.

Because this program is designed for younger retreatants who come with a lot of energy, the schedule is filled with structured activities. The structure helps to channel the energy in a positive fashion.

Goals

The goals of this retreat are the following:
- That the retreatants learn the meaning of traditional Advent symbols in order to more fully participate in the liturgical season of Advent
- That the retreatants examine ways to see Jesus in others
- That the retreatants reflect on the Virgin Mary's role in the life of Jesus and in their own life

Schedule

Day 1

9:30 a.m.	Arrival
10:00 a.m.	Introduction and prayer
10:45 a.m.	Icebreakers
11:30 a.m.	Small group 1: Getting acquainted and goal setting
12:15 p.m.	Lunch
1:00 p.m.	Recreation
2:00 p.m.	Quiet time
2:15 p.m.	Film or presentation
2:45 p.m.	Small group 2: Discussion
3:45 p.m.	Break
4:15 p.m.	Plan skits
5:15 p.m.	Advent songs
6:00 p.m.	Dinner
7:00 p.m.	Perform skits
8:45 p.m.	Break
9:15 p.m.	Reconciliation
10:30 p.m.	Fireside recreation
11:15 p.m.	Closedown

Day 2

7:45 a.m.	Wake-up call
8:30 a.m.	Breakfast
9:15 a.m.	Cleanup
10:00 a.m.	Morning prayer
10:45 a.m.	Break
11:00 a.m.	Small group 3: Closure
12:15 p.m.	Lunch
1:30 p.m.	Liturgy
2:45 p.m.	Wrap-up
3:00 p.m.	Departure

Materials needed for this retreat: blank name tags; food for two lunches, snacks, a breakfast, and a dinner; an Advent wreath; the song "Come, O Lord"; felt-tip markers; butcher paper; masking tape; the film *Martin the Cobbler;* a 16-mm film projector; a screen; Bibles; materials for skit props, such as glue, scissors, pencils, construction paper, and color markers; Advent songbooks; copies of handouts; writing materials; a tape or a record of instrumental music; and a record or tape player (See also the section "Materials Generally Needed for a Retreat" on page 16 of this manual.)

Retreat Activities: Day 1

9:30 a.m. Arrival

Two staff members welcome and register the retreatants, help them locate their room, and have them fill out their name tag.

10:00 a.m. Introduction and prayer

The introduction is a time to welcome the retreatants and to help them feel more comfortable. These younger retreatants will have a lot of nervous energy. Explaining the schedule and inviting questions during this time helps make the retreatants more comfortable.

Staff: two people. All staff members need to be present for introductions.

Materials needed: an Advent wreath with the appropriate number of candles lit, the song "Come, O Lord" from the album *Remember Your Love,* by Damean Music (If you cannot recruit a retreatant or a staff member who plays an instrument to lead the song, bring a tape or a record of the song and a tape or record player.)

Description of activities

1. Introduction: Say something like the following to introduce the theme of the retreat: "Advent is a time to prepare to receive Jesus into our heart. In the Scriptures, John the Baptist calls out to 'make straight the way of the Lord!' [John 1:23].

"Over the years, songs and traditions have been created to help us remember and prepare for the coming of Jesus.

"The Advent wreath is a visual way to express the meaning of the Advent season. Each of the four candles is for each Sunday in Advent. We light the candles to remind ourselves that Jesus is the light of the world. Three of the four candles are purple.

On the third Sunday of Advent, we light the pink or rose candle to express our joy that Christmas is so close. The wreath is made of evergreens placed in the shape of a circle. The evergreens are a reminder that God never changes, and the circular shape reminds us that God is eternal.

"Throughout this retreat you will have the opportunity to examine how the coming of Jesus today is similar in many ways to when he first came two thousand years ago. I wonder if you would recognize Jesus coming to you today. You will also have the opportunity to look at the role that Mary played in the life of Jesus and how her relationship with God can help us reflect on our own.

"As we begin this retreat, let's pray in song, asking Jesus to bring us peace."

2. Song: Teach the song "Come, O Lord" from the album *Remember Your Love* (Damean Music, 1978). If you have arranged for a retreatant or a staff member who is a musician to lead the song, teach the retreatants the refrain and have the musician sing the verses. If no musician is available, encourage the retreatants to sing along with a recording of the music.

3. Orientation: Explain the guidelines for using the facility and introduce the staff.

4. Getting acquainted: Invite the retreatants to introduce themselves to at least three people that they do not already know. Have the staff mingle with the group so that retreatants can introduce themselves to the staff if they do not know them.

10:45 a.m. Icebreakers

Staff: one person. Encourage all staff members to participate.

Materials needed: none

Description of activities

1. Introduction: Explain that the purpose of the icebreakers is to help the retreatants relax and feel more at ease with one another. Ask the retreatants to participate with a spirit of cooperation and playfulness. Give directions for the icebreakers two times. Ask if any retreatants need further clarification before you begin the activity.

2. Amoeba tag: This tag game is played entirely in slow motion. Designate someone in the group to be "It." The person who is It chases in slow motion another person in the group who also moves in slow motion. When the second person is caught, that person links arms with the person who caught him or her, and they become It together. They are now an "amoeba" on the prowl. They chase and catch in slow motion a third person who becomes part of the amoeba. When a fourth person is chased and caught, the amoeba splits and each pair becomes an amoeba on the prowl. This cycle is repeated until everyone is part of an amoeba.

When everyone has become part of an amoeba, it is time for the amoeba chant. This chant should be practiced before the icebreaker starts. The chant goes like this: A! ME! BA!!! Either the leader or one of the amoebas should start the chant very softly. When other amoebas hear the chant, they join in and begin to move together into a giant amoeba, bringing the chant to a final crescendo, which signals the end of the icebreaker.

3. Imaginary ball toss: Direct the group to stand in a circle. The leader then imagines that she or he has a tennis ball in one hand. The ball is demonstrated by closing the fist of the hand without the ball and not being able to close the fist holding the imaginary ball.

The leader then calls out someone's name and throws the ball to that person. The person who catches the ball then does the same thing that the leader did, that is, calls out the name of another person and throws the imaginary ball to that person. If names are not known, simply ask the name of the person intended to receive the ball, then call out the name and throw the imaginary ball. After the third or fourth toss, the leader interrupts and changes the name of the object that is to be thrown, for example, "Jerry, it is no longer a tennis ball, it is a watermelon." The leader also tells the group that from now on they can change the name of the object to be thrown to whatever they want it to be. The catching of the imaginary object should correspond to the type of imaginary object that is being thrown.

After everyone in the group has caught and thrown the imaginary object, a second round begins with people trying to remember the names of people without having to ask.

4. Summary: Ask the retreatants what their reactions to the icebreakers are. Comment on the activity, noting that the icebreakers were successful because the retreatants were working together. Encourage them to continue to bring this spirit of cooperation to each of the retreat activities. Assign small groups for the next activity.

11:30 a.m. Small group 1: Getting acquainted and goal setting

This small-group session is important for setting the tone of the retreat. Discussion guidelines will be established, which will be used during all the small-group sessions. Also, having the retreatants set a personal goal for the retreat challenges them to make a special effort to work in a particular direction during the retreat. The icebreakers were a playful activity. This discussion group is meant to be a more serious activity.

Staff: one person for each small group

Materials needed: felt-tip markers, butcher paper, and masking tape

Description of activities

1. Introductions: Invite everyone to introduce themselves to the group by giving their name and some unique characteristic about themselves.

2. Guidelines: Help the retreatants establish discussion guidelines and post them for all to see (see page 40).

3. Personal retreat goals: Invite the retreatants to think about why they came on the retreat. Encourage them to set a personal goal for the retreat. Suggest that the goal be related to the season of Advent. This goal will give them a specific direction in which to focus throughout the retreat.

Invite the retreatants to share their goal with the small-group members. After they have shared their goal orally, give the retreatants time to rethink their goal in light of their sharing. Then list these goals on butcher paper and save the list for use during small group 3.

4. Summary: Summarize the group's discussion. Invite everyone to make a closing comment. The younger participants might find this difficult to do so early in the retreat. It is not mandatory that everyone say something.

5. Closure: Invite a retreatant from the group to offer a closing prayer. Explain the schedule for the afternoon.

12:15 p.m. Lunch

One staff person should be available to make announcements and to choose a retreatant to lead the group in prayer before the meal.

1:00 p.m. Recreation

This time is scheduled to give the retreatants the opportunity to recreate. Encourage them to go outside during this time. Have recreational equipment available.

2:00 p.m. Quiet time

After a recreational period, it is difficult for the retreatants to refocus themselves and to begin a serious activity. So during this time, invite the retreatants to quiet themselves and to refocus their attention on the retreat goal they set during the morning small-group session.

Staff: one person to explain the activity

Materials needed: none

Description of activities

1. Explain that the purpose of the activity is to relax physically and to refocus on the goal for the retreat.

2. Invite the retreatants to find a comfortable position. Encourage the flat-on-back position with legs not crossed and arms at the side with the palms facing down and eyes closed.

3. As the retreatants settle down and begin to relax, encourage them to breathe slowly and deeply. Speaking softly, ask the retreatants to recall the personal retreat goal they set for themselves during the first small-group discussion. Encourage them to think about what they might need to do to accomplish this goal.

4. Be still for about ten minutes, allowing the retreatants to continue to relax and to think about their retreat goal.

5. Speaking softly, introduce the retreatants to the next activity.

2:15 p.m. Film or presentation

Choose one of the following two options for this segment of the retreat.

Option 1: Film—*Martin the Cobbler*

The film *Martin the Cobbler* is an adaptation of Leo Tolstoy's short story "Where Love Is, God Is." The characters are animated clay figures. This is an enjoyable way for the younger retreatants to reflect on the ways that Jesus comes to us.

Staff: two people (including one person to assist in operating the movie projector)

Materials needed: a 16-mm projector, a screen, the film *Martin the Cobbler* (thirty minutes), distributed by Billy Budd Films, 235 East Fifty-seventh Street, New York, NY 10022; phone 212-755-3968. Most diocesan religious education offices have this film available for rental

Description of activities: Introduce the film with words like the following: "I am going to show you a film about a cobbler. Martin lives and works in a small Russian village. As the story begins, Martin is very sad. He says, 'God and I have not been getting on well.'

"The Lord speaks to Martin telling him to look in the street 'for tomorrow I shall come.' During the introduction to the retreat, you were asked if you would be able to recognize Jesus if he came to you. View the film with that same question in mind."

Option 2: Presentation on recognizing Jesus in others

Use this option if the film is not available.

Staff: one person

Materials needed: a Bible

Description of activities

1. Introduce the activity with words like the following: "During this presentation I invite you to reflect on ways that Jesus comes to us. Have you ever wondered if you would be able to recognize Jesus if he came to you today? I wonder this sometimes too.

"There is a passage in the Scriptures that reminds me that Jesus comes to me through others. I am sure that you have heard this before today."

2. Read Matt. 25:31–46.

3. Give personal examples of times you felt that Jesus came to you through the kindness of others.

4. Give personal examples of when it was difficult for you to reach out in kindness to others.

5. Summarize the presentation and invite the retreatants to reflect on ways that they might bring Jesus to others, especially during the season of Advent.

2:45 p.m. Small group 2: Discussion

Two options are offered for this small-group session. If you showed the film, follow up with option 1 below. If you gave a presentation, use option 2.

Option 1: Film discussion

Staff: one person for each small group

Materials needed: none

Description of activities

1. Guidelines: Review the discussion guidelines established during the first small-group session.

2. Discussion: Discuss the film, using the following questions. Make sure that everyone gets an opportunity to respond to at least one of the questions.

- What part of the film do you remember most clearly?
- What part of the film did you like best? Why?

- Martin blamed the Lord for taking his family from him. Can you recall a time when you blamed the Lord when bad things happened to you? Give examples.
- Martin stated, "If the Lord were my guest, I would give him all the signs of welcome." Yet later the Lord asked, "Martin, do you not know me?" What makes it easy for you to recognize the Lord in people around you? What makes this difficult for you?
- Can you recall a time when you felt that Jesus came to you through the kindness of others?
- How might you bring Jesus to others in your life, especially during this Advent time? Give examples of how you might do this at school, at home, and in your city.
- How might you more deeply prepare, during this Advent time, to receive Jesus when he comes?

3. Summary: Summarize the discussion. Invite all group members to make a closing comment.

4. Closure: Invite a retreatant to offer a closing prayer.

Option 2: Discussion of presentation

Staff: one person for each small group

Materials needed: none

Description of activities

1. Guidelines: Review the discussion guidelines established during the first small-group meeting.

2. Discussion: Discuss the presentation. Begin by going around the room asking each retreatant to answer the first question given below. After everyone has answered the first question, point out the similarities and differences in their responses. Continue facilitating the discussion, using the rest of the questions.
- When you think of Jesus, what image comes to your mind?
- What experience of yours has influenced you in forming this image of Jesus?
- How did you feel when you heard the scriptural passage that was read during the presentation?
- Is there anything in that passage that confuses you? If so, what?
- Have you ever felt that Jesus came to you through the kindness of others?
- How might you bring Jesus to others in your life, especially during this Advent time? Give examples of how you might do this at school, at home, and in your city.

3. Summary: Summarize the discussion. Invite all group members to make a closing comment.

4. Closure: Invite a retreatant to offer a closing prayer.

3:45 p.m. Break

4:15 p.m. Plan skits

This activity is designed to help the retreatants understand more deeply what they discussed in their small group. The leader introduces the activity and supervises the retreatants as they plan skits that reflect ways in which Jesus comes to us today.

Staff: one person for each small group

Materials needed: materials with which to make props, such as pencils, construction paper, scissors, glue, and color markers

Description of activities

1. Introduce the skits by saying something like the following: "We often view the coming of Jesus as an event that took place two thousand years ago, so we may think that it doesn't really mean much today. During the last small-group discussion, you looked at ways that Jesus does come to us today. This activity is a follow-up to your discussion.

"Each small group will plan and perform a skit portraying a way in which Jesus comes today—a modern Christmas story. These will be planned now and performed after dinner. Be as creative as you can."

2. Explain where the materials for props are and ask the retreatants if they need further clarification. Rather than giving too many specific examples about what to do, encourage their creativity.

3. The retreatants plan skits.

4. Direct the retreatants to move their props to an assigned place.

5:15 p.m. Advent songs

Choose one of the following options for this segment of the retreat.

Option 1: Songfest

During this activity, the leader leads the retreatants in song as a way to unite them as a community and to remind them of the meaning of the Advent season. Having a songfest at this time is an enjoyable way to help the retreatants reflect on our Advent traditions as well as to unite the group. Song has a tendency to do that.

Staff: one person to lead the singing. All staff members should be present.

Materials needed: Advent songbooks

Description of activities: Remind the retreatants of the stories of Jesus that we pass on through our songs. Use spiritually oriented songs during this activity (e.g., "Away in a Manger" and "O Little Town of Bethlehem"). Later in the evening, traditional seasonal songs may be sung.

Option 2: Song lists

Divide the retreatants into groups of five. Have each group list as many religious Advent and Christmas songs as they can (up to fifteen). Each song needs to start with a different letter, and the group has to be able to sing a verse of one of the songs for their list to qualify.

If there is a tie for the longest list, the group that best performs in singing a verse of one of their songs is declared champion of song.

6:00 p.m. Dinner

One staff person should be available to make announcements and to choose a retreatant to lead the group in grace before the meal.

7:00 p.m. Perform skits

Staff: one person to coordinate the activity and all small-group leaders to assist their group members

Materials needed: the props prepared by the retreatants and writing materials

Description of activities

1. *Introduction:* Explain that the purpose of performing these skits is to give the retreatants an opportunity to reflect on ways Jesus comes to us today. Distribute writing materials.

2. *Skits:* Invite the small groups to perform their skits.

3. *Feedback:* After each skit is performed, ask the other retreatants to write down some feedback—what they liked about the skit and whether Jesus ever came to them in the way the skit portrayed his coming. After all the skits are performed, have the retreatants read their feedback to each group.

4. *Closure:* Invite the retreatants to make any closing comments about the activity.

8:45 p.m. Break

9:15 p.m. Reconciliation

Staff: one leader and several priests, depending on the number of retreatants

Materials needed: background music, a record or tape player, and handout 7-A

Description of activities

1. *Introduction and prayer:* Distribute handout 7-A, "Reconciliation." Introduce this activity with words like the following: "We have spent a lot of time today seeing how Jesus does come to us through others. We all forget this at times. To continue in our Advent preparation, let's pray that Jesus will open our heart.

"Come, Lord Jesus. Prepare us to celebrate your birthday. Your love and forgiveness are the greatest gifts we receive at Christmas. We pray that we might open our heart to receive you. We pray this in your name, Lord Jesus."

2. *Reading:* Matt. 3:1-12 and a reflection on the reading

3. *Examination of conscience and communal prayer of contrition:* Refer the retreatants to handout 7-A for both of these remaining parts of the liturgy.

4. *Confessions:* Indicate to the retreatants the priest (or priests) who will be hearing confessions. Tell them that if they wish to discuss something in greater depth than time allows, the priest will be available later as well.

5. *Closure:* The priest invites the group to join in singing the Lord's Prayer and in exchanging the sign of peace and concludes with a prayer and a blessing (see handout 7-A).

10:30 p.m. Fireside recreation

During this recreational period, have seasonal songbooks and snacks available. Encourage the retreatants to sing with or without accompaniment. All of the staff members should be present.

11:15 p.m. Closedown

One staff person explains the procedures for retiring and the schedule for the next day and makes any other necessary announcements. It is advisable to have an adult staff member supervise the closedown to assure that all the retreatants are safely retired.

Retreat Activities: Day 2

7:45 a.m. Wake-up call

8:30 a.m. Breakfast

One staff member should be available to choose a retreatant to lead the meal prayer and to choose retreatants to read the various parts of the prayer scheduled for 10:00 a.m.

9:15 a.m. Cleanup

This time allows the retreatants to change sheets, clean rooms, pack belongings, and load the cars or the bus in preparation for departure. One staff person should explain the activity. All staff members should help supervise the activity.

10:00 a.m. Morning prayer

This activity uses the joyful mysteries of the rosary to give the retreatants an opportunity to reflect on their relationship with God in light of Mary's relationship with God and Jesus.

Staff: two people (the retreat leader and one person to help distribute handouts)

Materials needed: Bibles, pencils, background music, a record or tape player, and handout 7–B

Description of activities

1. Introduction: "During this morning's prayer, we are going to take some time to prayerfully reflect on Mary's role in Jesus' life. Throughout the centuries, the Church has considered this important. Mary has the title Mother of the Church. Mary is also the patron of the United States.

"Advent is an appropriate time to reflect on Mary's role in Jesus' life. At the same time that we prepare to celebrate the birth of Jesus, we also celebrate Mary, his mother. On 8 December, the feast of the Immaculate Conception, we remember the uniqueness of Mary—that she was conceived without original sin.

"A devotion that has been practiced in our Church is to reflect on the events of Mary's life while praying the joyful mysteries of the rosary. This morning you will have time to read some passages in the Scriptures that refer to these events.

"My hope is that in prayerfully reading the Scriptures, you might be able to understand more fully how much Mary trusted in God and made many sacrifices in her life to follow God's will for her. She is a model of one who centered her life around Jesus. Mary can help us walk with Jesus."

2. The Joyful Mysteries: Pass out pencils; handout 7–B, "The Joyful Mysteries of the Rosary"; and Bibles. Read the directions on the handout with the retreatants and select readers. Proceed with the readings and the reflections as directed on the handout. Play background music during the activity. After the retreatants have written their reflections on the last reading, invite them to read or comment on any reflections.

3. Prayer: As a closing prayer, invite the retreatants to quietly read the Magnificat (Luke 1:46–55), which is on the handout.

4. Closure: Collect the Bibles and make closing comments.

Optional activity: Prepare an outline of a five-decade rosary on the floor. Place a basket with a sign for each joyful mystery of the rosary at the appropriate place on the outline.

After reflections on the joyful mysteries have been completed, ask the retreatants to cut their reflections from the handouts and place them in the baskets corresponding to each of the joyful mysteries. Invite the retreatants to read these reflections at their leisure, making sure to return reflections to their proper basket.

10:45 a.m. Break

11:00 a.m. Small group 3: Closure

This small group is designed to help the retreatants put closure on their retreat experience. By reviewing their goal, they have the opportunity to take personal responsibility for the retreat experience. By forming resolutions, the retreatants are challenged to take from the retreat some specific intentions to help deepen their Advent experience.

Staff: one person for each small group

Materials needed: retreat goals from the first small-group session

Description of activities

1. Review retreat goals: Present the list of goals discussed and written down during the first small-group session. Ask each retreatant to locate their own goal on the list and to explain any progress they have made in working toward this goal.

2. Resolutions: Invite the retreatants to share some of the reflections they wrote during the morning prayer. Have the retreatants formulate a resolution based on their reflections that will help to keep alive the meaning of the season of Advent. Advise them to keep the resolutions possible and practical.

3. Liturgical preparation: Ask each group to choose a representative to assist with the liturgical

responsibilities. (The groups that do the Prayer of the Faithful and the presentation of offertory gifts could have more than one representative.) Below is a list of suggested assignments.
- proclaiming the first reading: Isa. 9:1-6
- reading the response, "I will bless the Lord at all times," with Ps. 34:2-3,4-5,6-7,8-9,10-11
- proclaiming the second reading: Titus 2:11-14
- offering the Prayer of the Faithful
- presenting the offertory gifts

    4. Closure: End with a prayer.

12:15 p.m. Lunch

One staff person should be available to make announcements and to choose a retreatant to lead the group in prayer before the meal.

1:30 p.m. Liturgy

The group representatives carry out those parts of the liturgy for which they are responsible. An appropriate gospel reading would be John 1:6-9,19-28

2:45 p.m. Wrap-up

    Staff: one person (the same person who lead the introduction and prayer in the morning)

Materials needed: none

Description of activities: "During this retreat you have had the opportunity to reflect on the meaning of Advent. We have discussed ways that Jesus comes to us and how we often just do not see him when he is right before us. Together we have celebrated the Sacrament of Reconciliation. You have prayerfully reflected on Mary's life with Jesus, as well as your own and made some resolutions to take with you as you leave this retreat.

"I challenge you to keep these resolutions alive. There will be many distractions that will make it easy to forget what you have learned these two days on retreat. Spend time reading the Scriptures as you prepare to celebrate the birthday of Jesus. Call upon Jesus to assist you in this preparation. I encourage you to pray for one another."

Make any necessary announcements, such as the procedure for departure, the location for taking a group picture, and the date of the retreat follow-up.

3:00 p.m. Departure

Reconciliation

Examination of Conscience

Priest: Let us pray. God, we are your people, made one with you by your own son; as we come to celebrate the wonders of your merciful forgiveness, help us to examine our consciences that we might acknowledge our sinfulness with humility and contrition. We ask this through Jesus Christ our Lord.

All: Amen.

Leader: Let us listen to words of the Lord from the Scriptures, and as we listen, ask forgiveness for times when we have failed to live God's word.
"If you forgive others their failings, God will forgive yours; but if you do not forgive others, God will not forgive yours either" (Matthew 6:14–15).

All: Lord, we fail to acknowledge your presence when we sin against our brothers and sisters. Forgive us for those times we have failed to forgive our brothers and sisters, for times when we have harbored grudges in our heart, for times when we have chosen to be petty and selfish.

Leader: "No one can be the slave of two masters: either he will hate the first and love the second, or treat the first with respect and the second with scorn. You cannot be the slave of both God and money" (Matthew 6:24).

All: Lord, we fail to recognize your presence when we are too attached to our possessions. Forgive us for being too concerned about things of this world; for being selfish with the gifts you have given us; for failing to respond to the needs of our poor brothers and sisters.

Leader: "I say this to you: love your enemies and pray for those who persecute you" (Matthew 5:44).

All: Forgive us Lord, for failing to trust in the power of your healing Spirit; for failing to respond with love when we receive rejection.

Communal Prayer of Contrition

Priest: Let us together confess our sinfulness.

All: I confess to almighty God, and to you, my sisters and brothers, that I have sinned through my own fault in what I have done and in what I have failed to do. And I ask blessed Mary, ever virgin, all the angels and saints, and you, my sisters and brothers, to pray for me to the Lord our God.

Priest: May almighty God have mercy on us, forgive us our sins, and bring us to life everlasting.

All: Amen.

Private Confessions

All: [While others are going for individual confession, use your time to reflect, to write in your journal, or to pray quietly.]

Communal Penance

Priest: As our penance, let us pray together in the way that Jesus taught us.

All: [Recite or sing the Lord's Prayer.]

Priest: Lord Jesus Christ, you said to your Apostles: I leave you peace, my peace I give you. Look not on our sins, but on the faith of your Church, and grant us the peace and unity of your kingdom where you live forever and ever.

All: Amen.

Priest: As a sign of our reconciliation with God and with one another, let us offer each other a sign of peace.

All: [Exchange a sign of peace.]

Concluding Prayer and Blessing

Priest: Lord, hear the prayers of all who call upon you, forgive the sins of those who confess to you, and in your merciful love, give us your pardon and your peace. This we ask through Christ our Lord.

All: Amen.

Priest: May almighty God bless us, the Father, the Son, and the Holy Spirit.

All: Amen.

Priest: This celebration of God's forgiveness is now finished, let us go in peace.

All: Amen.

(Adapted from *Today's Missal,* vol. 54, no. 3:52)

The Joyful Mysteries of the Rosary

The joyful mysteries of the rosary commemorate Mary's intimate relationship with Jesus and God. We will use the scriptural passages on which these mysteries are based, plus some commentaries, to reflect on our life and our relationship with God.

For each of the five mysteries, we will (a) read the scriptural passage listed, (b) read the modern-day commentary, (c) quietly reflect on the scriptural passage and commentary, and (d) write personal reflections in the space provided.

1. The Annunciation

Reader 1: Luke 1:26–38 (Pause.)

Reader 2: This is a time when we can think about what was happening to Mary. The angel Gabriel was asking Mary to do something that she did not understand. At times in our life, we are asked to do things that we do not understand. Yet Mary trusted in God. Her words were, "Be it done unto me according to your word." There will not always be an answer or a reason.

The angel was a messenger from God. Through people and events in our life, God is able to reveal to us what it is that we are to do. Perhaps this can be a time when we reflect on how God communicates with us.

Pause for reflection: How might I better listen to God? What events in my life have shown me God's will? Who reminds me of God's will in my life?

▽ **Write your reflections.**

2. The Visitation

Reader 3: Luke 1:39–56 (Pause.)

Reader 4: Mary was sharing her joy with her cousin Elizabeth. They were celebrating the upcoming birth of the Child. Mary is an example of someone who goes out of her way to visit another. She does not just sit around and worry about her own situation.

Pause for reflection: When do you feel like celebrating? Who do you want to be with you? Who has gone out of their way to be with you in joyful and sorrowful times? Whom have you gone to for help?

▽ **Write your reflections.**

3. The Birth of Jesus

Reader 5: Luke 2:1–7 (Pause.)

Reader 6: The birth of Jesus is the time when the Word was made flesh. The Word of God, who is Jesus, came into the world. Jesus still comes to us through the love of other people.

Pause for reflection: What happens to you when you know you are loved? When have others treated you lovingly? How can you help others to know the love of Jesus? Have you thanked God for the loving persons you know?

▽ **Write your reflections.**

4. Presentation of Jesus in the Temple

Reader 7: Luke 2:22–40 (Pause.)

Reader 8: Mary and Joseph took Jesus to the Temple to fulfill the Jewish custom. The firstborn son was to be offered to God. Mary and Joseph had already offered Jesus to God in their heart, but they respected the custom and the value of the ritual in their life. So they brought Jesus.

Pause for reflection: Try to recall times in your life when you participated in a ritual that did not make a whole lot of sense to you. Did you quickly pass it off as something that was not important or were you able to learn to appreciate the value of ritual and tradition in your life?

▽ **Write your reflections.**

5. The Finding of Jesus in the Temple

Reader 9: Luke 2:41–52 (Pause.)

Reader 10: Imagine the fear that overcame Mary and Joseph when they realized that their son was lost. When they found Jesus, they asked him why he had done this. Jesus knew what he was to be doing for God. Even so, he returned to Nazareth with Mary and Joseph and was obedient to them. Even Jesus was misunderstood. Yet in the midst of a misunderstanding, his behavior showed the love and respect due his parents.

Pause for reflection: When have your parents worried about you because you were not home at a particular time? Does your behavior toward your parents reflect the love and respect due them?

▽ **Write your reflections.**

The Magnificat

My being proclaims your greatness,
and my spirit finds joy in you, God my Savior.
For you have looked upon me, your servant, in my lowliness;
all ages to come shall call me blessed.

God, you who are mighty, have done great things for me.
Holy is your name.

Your mercy is from age to age toward those who fear you.

You have shown might with your arm
and confused the proud in their inmost thoughts.

You have deposed the mighty from their thrones
and raised the lowly to high places.

The hungry you have given every good thing
while the rich you have sent away empty.

You have upheld Israel your servant, ever mindful of your mercy—

even as you promised our ancestors;
promised Abraham, Sarah, and their descendants forever.

(Luke 1:46–55)

8 ▽

Change My Heart, O God: An Alcohol and Drug Abuse Prevention Retreat

"Change My Heart, O God" is a two-day retreat directed at alcohol and drug abuse. The program can accommodate ten to forty high-school-age people. The program can be beneficial for retreatants who have never misused drugs as well as for persons who are currently struggling with an abuse problem.

Most young people have been exposed to the effects of alcohol and drug abuse through either their own substance abuse or that of family members, friends, classmates, or public figures. On this retreat, the young people will discover constructive means of handling the pressure and the decisions they face with regard to the use of alcohol or drugs and other daily concerns. The activities focus on problem-solving techniques, social skills, and the clarification of personal values and goals.

Goals

The goals of this retreat are the following:
- That the retreatants examine their attitudes toward alcohol and drug use
- That the retreatants learn about the harmful effects of substance abuse by listening to the experiences of a panel of recovering adolescents
- That the retreatants learn how to respond with effective Christian behavior to stressful situations that could lead to alcohol or substance abuse

Additional Information for Staff Members

Research in the area of alcohol and drug abuse has shown that the use of alcohol and drugs can be lethal. Alcohol poisons the central nervous system. Opiates suppress the heart rate and respiratory system. Cocaine affects the central nervous system as well as the heart.

Alcohol erodes the body's systems and causes premature aging. This damage happens ten times faster in young people than it does in adults. On the other hand, young people also heal faster than adults.

Next to PCP (phencyclidine), marijuana is the most brain-damaging drug. Liver damage also can result from marijuana use. Liver disease, in turn, enhances the chance of cancer.

Addiction (alcoholism, drug addiction, etc.) can be defined as a disease, specifically, a psychobiological disease with a genetic predisposition. Genetic predisposition for an addiction occurs randomly. Once the predisposition for alcoholism is established in a family, a child in that family has four times as many chances of becoming alcoholic.

Note: Because this retreat raises sensitive issues, it is imperative that a counseling referral list be available to the staff and the retreatants.

Schedule

Day 1

9:30 a.m.	Arrival
10:00 a.m.	Introduction and prayer
10:30 a.m.	Icebreakers
11:15 a.m.	Small group 1: Goal setting
12:00 m.	Lunch
1:00 p.m.	Videotape: *My Father's Son*
1:30 p.m.	Small group 2: Discussion of the videotape
2:30 p.m.	Recreation
4:00 p.m.	Progressive relaxation
4:30 p.m.	Role-play
6:00 p.m.	Dinner
7:15 p.m.	Panel of recovering adolescents
8:45 p.m.	Break
9:30 p.m.	Reconciliation
11:00 p.m.	Break
11:30 p.m.	Closedown

Day 2

7:45 a.m.	Wake-up call
8:00 a.m.	Breakfast
8:45 a.m.	Cleanup
9:30 a.m.	Morning prayer
10:30 a.m.	Small group 3: Closure
12:15 p.m.	Lunch
1:30 p.m.	Liturgy
2:45 p.m.	Wrap-up
3:00 p.m.	Departure

Before the retreat

- Contact a local young people's Alcoholics Anonymous (AA) or Narcotics Anonymous (NA) group and arrange for recovering abusers to be part of a panel that speaks to the retreatants.
- Prepare a counseling referral list that includes meeting times and telephone numbers of AA, NA, Cocaine Anonymous (CA), Al-Anon, and Alateen.
- Type on slips of paper the scenarios used in the role-play activity (see page 70).

Materials needed for this retreat: the song "Change My Heart"; food for a breakfast, a lunch, breaks, and a dinner; two small balls; felt-tip markers; butcher paper; masking tape; the videotape *My Father's Son;* a video camera; a video recorder; a blank videotape; a TV monitor; copies of a counseling referral list; recreational equipment; a Bible; a tape or a record of instrumental music, a tape or record player; writing materials; and a candle

Retreat Activities: Day 1

9:30 a.m. Arrival

Two staff members welcome and register the retreatants, help them locate their room, and have them fill out a name tag.

10:00 a.m. Introduction and prayer

The introduction is a time to welcome the retreatants and to help them feel more comfortable as they begin the retreat. Some of the retreatants will be apprehensive because the retreat topic is a sensitive one. Explaining the schedule and inviting questions during this time can help make the retreatants more comfortable.

Staff: one person. All staff members need to be present for introductions.

Materials needed: "Change My Heart" from the album *Praise 9*, by Maranatha Music (If you cannot recruit a retreatant or a staff member who plays an instrument to lead the song, bring a tape or a record of the song and a tape or record player.)

Description of activities

1. Introduction: Say something like the following to introduce the theme of the retreat: "All of you have been exposed in some way to the effects of alcohol and drug abuse. Some of you have family members who struggle with a problem in this area. Some of you know friends or classmates who use drugs. If you do not know of any family members, friends, or classmates who abuse alcohol or drugs, you have probably heard about alcohol and drug abuse in the news or seen the effects of it in movies and on TV commercials.

"During this retreat, you will have the chance to examine your own attitudes toward alcohol and drug use. To assist you in examining your attitudes, a number of activities are planned. You will view and discuss a videotape, participate in role-playing, and listen to a panel of young people share with you their own experiences of recovering from alcohol and drug abuse.

"The theme of this retreat moves us to turn our heart to God in Jesus and asks God to change our heart to a direction that is a way of life closer to God's loving way. Sometimes in our life we are alone; we are powerless. At these times of powerlessness, I encourage you to call out to God in prayer and ask for that change of heart. As our heart changes and we move closer to God, we will experience the peace of God that Jesus gives. My hope for you during this retreat is that you will know more of the great love God in Jesus has for you and that knowing his love, you will be willing to let your heart be changed."

2. Song: Teach the song "Change My Heart" from the album *Praise 9,* by Maranatha Music. If you have arranged for a retreatant or a staff member who is a musician to lead the song, teach the retreatants the refrain and have the musician sing the verses. If no musician is available, encourage the retreatants to sing along with a recording of the music. Because the refrain is simple, no songbooks are necessary.

3. Orientation: Explain the guidelines for using the facility and introduce the staff.

4. Getting acquainted: Invite the retreatants to introduce themselves to two other people in the group that they do not know. Encourage the staff to mingle with the group and be part of these introductions.

10:30 a.m. Icebreakers

Staff: one person (Encourage all staff members to participate.)

Materials needed: two small balls

Description of activities

1. Introduction: Explain that the purpose of the icebreakers is to help the retreatants relax and feel more at ease with one another. Give directions for the icebreakers. For each activity, explain the directions two times. Ask the retreatants if they have any questions.

2. A What? Arrange the retreatants in a circle, facing the center. One person takes a ball and hands it to the person on the right saying, "This is a banana." Person 2 says, "A what?" and person 1 says, "A banana." Person 2 then gives the ball to the person on the right and says, "This is a banana." Person 3 says, "A what?" and person 2 turns back to person 1 and says, "A what?" Person 1 says again, "A banana." Person 2 turns to person 3 and says, "A banana." Person 3 then gives the ball to person 4 on the right and the whole sequence repeats from person 4 to person 1 and back again.

Meanwhile, person 1 gives another ball to the person on the left and says, "This is a pineapple." And the pineapple ball takes off to the left with the same sequence of "a what" and "a pineapple."

If the group is not totally confused by the time the banana and pineapple collide and pass each other, more fruit can be added to the circle.

3. Shoe factory: Arrange the retreatants in a circle, facing the center. Have them all take off their shoes and place them in a pile in the center of the circle. Then everyone takes three steps to the pile and selects a pair of unmatched shoes, neither of which are their own, and puts them on.

Next, chanting "shoe, shoe, shoe," they shuffle around trying to find the persons wearing the mates to their shoes. When the mates to the shoes are found, the players stand with the matching feet together so that all the shoes are in proper pairs. The players will have worked themselves into some kind of circle by now, and they can slip out of their shoes, leaving them in matched pairs for the owners to claim.

4. Rain: Arrange the group sitting in a circle, facing the center. Tell everyone to close their eyes and to get ready to repeat the sound that the person on their right will be making. The leader begins by rubbing the palms of his or her hands together to make a sound like drizzle. The person to the left joins in, and then the next person to the left, and so on, with the drizzle sound increasing in intensity.

When the drizzle sound has made it around the circle to the leader, with the entire circle rubbing their palms, the leader begins to change the drizzle to a sprinkle by snapping his or her fingers. The sprinkling rain replaces the drizzle by moving around the circle, increasing in intensity.

Next the leader changes the sprinkle to a hard rain by clapping, then to a downpour by slapping his or her thighs, and finally to a storm by getting everyone to stomp their feet.

Then the storm begins to subside by reversing the sequence of sound from foot stomping to thigh slapping to clapping to finger snapping to palm rubbing. When the drizzle stops, everyone joins hands and opens their eyes to the sunshine.

5. Summary: Comment on the activity, noting that the icebreakers were successful because everyone was working together. Encourage the group to bring this spirit of cooperation to all of the retreat activities. Assign small groups for the next activity.

11:15 p.m. Small group 1: Goal setting

This small group is an important activity as it sets the tone for the retreat. The discussion guidelines established in this session will be used throughout the retreat. The retreatants also set personal goals to work toward throughout the retreat.

Staff: one person for each small group

Materials needed: felt-tip markers, butcher paper, and masking tape

Description of activities

1. Guidelines: Help the retreatants establish discussion guidelines and post them for all to see (see page 40).

2. Introductions: Invite the participants to introduce themselves to the group by stating their name, their hobbies, and why they chose to come to this retreat.

3. Personal retreat goals: Invite the retreatants to reflect on the following question:
- Keeping in mind the topic of the retreat, what do you need most in your life at this time?

Allow a few minutes for the retreatants to reflect on this question. Encourage them to set a personal goal to give themselves a specific direction throughout the retreat.

Invite the retreatants to share their goal with the other small-group members. Some retreatants may not want to share their goal. Respect their choice.

4. Summary: Summarize the group session. Invite everyone to make a closing comment.

5. Closure: Invite a retreatant to offer a closing prayer and explain the schedule for the afternoon.

12:00 m. Lunch

One staff person should be available to make announcements and to choose a retreatant to lead the group in grace before the meal.

1:00 p.m. Videotape: *My Father's Son*

Up until now, the retreat activities have been relatively light. This activity will begin a serious approach to a serious subject. The videotape *My Father's Son* is a thirty-minute presentation about the hereditary effects of alcoholism. Make sure that the leader of this activity has previewed the videotape before this showing.

Staff: two people (including one to assist with the video recorder)

Materials needed: the videotape *My Father's Son* from Hazelden Educational Materials (Box 176 Center City, MN 55102; phone 800-328-9000), a video recorder, and a TV monitor.

Description of activities: Introduce the videotape. Give the title of the program and explain that the purpose of showing the videotape is to raise the issue of alcohol addiction. Because the video brings up the issue of the hereditary effects of alcoholism, do not discuss this in the introduction.

Encourage the retreatants to note the feelings they experience while viewing the video.

1:30 p.m. Small group 2: Discussion of the videotape

Denial is a common symptom of someone with an addiction, so some retreatants might demonstrate an indifferent or negative reaction to the videotape. Be sensitive to their feelings. Do not push. The important objective is to establish trust. Trust will be established by respecting the emotions of the retreatants. This is not a time to be confrontational. It is a time to create an environment conducive to an exploration of thoughts and feelings about substance abuse.

Staff: one person for each small group

Materials needed: none

Description of activities

1. Guidelines: Review the discussion guidelines established during the first small-group session, especially stressing the importance of confidentiality.

2. Discussion: Give the retreatants several minutes to think about the video, then lead a discussion using the following questions. After you ask the first question, tell the retreatants to turn to another person to share their answer. (This will help the retreatants to feel more at ease because they do not have to answer to the whole group.)

After the retreatants have discussed the first question with someone, ask if anyone is willing to tell the whole group how she or he answered the question. When the first question is answered, address the rest of the questions to the group as a whole.
- What feelings did you have while viewing the video?
- What did you like about the video?
- What did you dislike about the video?
- What concerns do you have about the hereditary aspect of addiction?
- What in your experience has influenced your feelings about this issue?
- What type of support do you need in this area?
- What type of support would you like to give others in this area?

3. Summary: Stress the importance of confidentiality for all that has been discussed. Invite each group member to make a closing comment.

4. Closure: Invite a retreatant to offer a closing prayer.

2:30 p.m. Recreation

Because the afternoon and the evening are full of serious activities, this recreational period is important. The retreatants can benefit from exercise and fresh air. Have recreational equipment such as volleyballs or Frisbees available. If the weather is inclement, you might use the Rain icebreaker (see page 67) as a group indoor-recreation activity.

4:00 p.m. Progressive relaxation

Besides teaching the retreatants a relaxation technique, this activity quiets them after the recreational period.

Staff: one person

Materials needed: none

Description of activities

1. Introduction: Explain that the purpose of the activity is to relax physically. Tell the retreatants that you will lead them through a process of relaxing various muscles and then allow a time for being quiet.

2. Progressive relaxation: Invite the retreatants to find a comfortable position. Encourage the flat-on-back position with legs not crossed and arms at the side with the palms facing down and eyes closed. Then lead the process with words like the following: "Direct your attention to your left hand. Clench it tightly and notice the tension in your hand and forearm. [Pause five seconds.] Now let go. Relax your left hand and let it rest on the floor. Notice the difference between the tension and the relaxation.

"Now do the same thing with your right hand. Clench your right fist. Notice the tension in your hand and forearm. [Pause five seconds.] Now let go. Relax your right hand and let it rest on the floor. Again, notice the difference between the tension and the relaxation.

"Bend both hands back at the wrists so you can tense the muscles in the back of the hand and in the forearm. Notice the tension. [Pause five seconds.] Now relax. Let your hands return to the resting position and notice the difference between the tension and the relaxation.

"Clench both of your hands into fists and bring them toward your shoulders so as to tighten the muscles in the upper part of your arm. [Pause five seconds.] Now relax. Return your arms to your sides. Notice the difference between the tension and the relaxation.

"Direct your attention to your shoulder area. Shrug your shoulders. Bring them up toward your ears. Notice the tension in your shoulders and neck. [Pause five seconds.] Now relax. Return both shoulders to their resting position. Notice the relaxation spreading through your shoulder area.

"Now relax the various muscles of your face. Wrinkle up your forehead and brow. [Pause five seconds.] Relax. Close your eyes tightly. Notice the tension in the many muscles around your eyes. [Pause five seconds.] Relax those muscles. Clench your jaw by biting your teeth together. Notice the tension in your jaw. [Pause five seconds.] Relax.

"Turn your attention to your neck. Press your head back against the floor. Notice the tension in your neck muscles. [Pause five seconds.] Relax. Bring your head forward to try to bury it in your chest. Feel the tension. [Pause five seconds.] Relax.

"Now direct your attention to the muscles in your upper back. Arch your back. Stick out your stomach and your chest. Notice the tension. [Pause five seconds.] Relax. Let those muscles become more and more loose.

"Now take a deep breath. Fill your lungs and hold it. Notice the tension in your chest and stomach area. Exhale. Relax. Continue breathing as you were. Notice the difference between the tension and the relaxation.

"Now tighten the muscles in your stomach. Make your stomach hard. [Pause five seconds.] Relax.

"Now stretch both legs. Stretch them so you can feel tension in your thighs. [Pause five seconds.] Relax and again notice the difference between the tension and the relaxation.

"Now tense your calf muscles by pointing your toes toward your head. Notice the tension of the muscles. [Pause five seconds.] Relax.

"Just as you have been directing your muscles to tense, you have also been directing them to relax or loosen. You have noted the difference between tension and relaxation. In noticing the tension in any of your muscles, you can try to concentrate on that part. Send messages to that muscle to loosen and relax. If you think you are loosening that muscle, you will in fact be able to do so.

"I will now review the various muscle groups that we covered. As I name each group, try to notice if there is any tension in those muscles. If you notice tension, try to concentrate on those muscles. Send them messages to relax.

"Relax the muscles in your feet [pause], ankles [pause], calves and shins [pause], knees and thighs [pause], buttocks and hips. [Pause.] Loosen the muscles of your lower body.

"Relax your stomach [pause], waist and lower back [pause], upper back, chest, and shoulders. [Pause.] Relax your upper arms [pause], forearms, right to the tips of your fingers. [Pause.] Let the muscles of your throat and neck loosen. [Pause.] Relax your jaw and facial muscles. [Pause.] Let all the muscles in your body become loose.

"Now lie quietly with your eyes closed. Do nothing more than that. You are going to relax your body and mind."

3. *Quiet time:* Allow for the quiet time. After ten minutes, gently invite the retreatants to turn their thoughts back to the retreat. Allow them to slowly return their attention to the leader. Remind the retreatants that they can use this relaxation technique any time to help cope with stressful situations, whether resulting from drug or alcohol abuse or other causes.

4:30 p.m. Role-Play

Young people daily face stressful situations that challenge their behavior. This activity is designed to help young people practice behaviors that are appropriate to various situations and in line with Christian values. Not all the scenarios relate directly to alcohol and drug abuse. Be sure to explain to the retreatants that practicing behavior in a variety of stressful situations prepares them to respond to stressful situations that might lead to alcohol and drug abuse.

Staff: two people (including one person to operate the video camera)

Materials needed: a video camera, a blank videotape, a TV monitor, and a video recorder

Description of activities

1. Introduce the activity by saying something like the following: "The purpose of this activity is to practice Christian-valued behaviors during potentially stressful situations. Practicing behavior in a variety of stressful situations prepares us to respond to stressful situations that might lead to alcohol and drug abuse.

"We will work in small groups, and each group will be given a scenario to act out. These will be videotaped. After the acting, the videotape will be reviewed by the whole group. Then we will discuss alternative ways to approach the situation. Decisions will be made by the group and the actors will replay the scenario. [The scenarios are from social, occupational, and educational areas because these are areas of concern to young people.]

"At first, the idea of being filmed may cause you to feel uneasy. Relax! Try to have fun with this."

2. Divide the retreatants into five groups and assign the following scenarios (distribute the scenarios typed on slips of paper):

Scenario 1: Dating
John and Sue are on their second date. Sue likes John and hopes to develop a deeper friendship. Sue feels uncomfortable, though, as John keeps pressuring her to physically express her care for him.

Note: During the discussion on alternative ways to act in this situation, encourage the direct expression of feelings and honest communication by Sue. Assertive behavior by Sue communicates that she and John have equal rights. Passive behavior by Sue communicates that John's rights are more important than hers. Aggressive behavior by John communicates that his rights are more important than Sue's.

Scenario 2: Employment
Nicole has been working at a fast-food restaurant for six months. Michael comes to work, visibly upset. His mother has been drinking heavily. Nicole approaches Michael because she is concerned about him.

Note: During the discussion on alternative ways to act in this situation, encourage the actors to make use of Al-Anon, Alateen, and counseling referrals.

Scenario 3: School
Tom is a popular senior. Jim observes Tom selling drugs to a freshman. Jim is concerned and discusses with Patty, his girlfriend, what he should do.

Note: During the discussion on alternative ways to act in this situation, encourage the actors to speak to appropriate adults in order to help Tom and the freshman in their substance-abuse problems.

Scenario 4: Dating
Tim likes Martha a lot. They have never met, yet he would like to take her on a date. Tim asks Chris what he should do.

Note: During the discussion on alternative ways to act in this situation, encourage honest communication and direct expression of feelings.

Scenario 5: Friends
Mary is new in town. She would like to join some of her classmates who are going out for pizza. Mary overhears the pizza-party conversation. She approaches the group in order to gain an invitation.

Note: During the discussion on alternative ways to act in this situation, encourage the actors to be sensitive to the needs of others (i.e., new people in town) and to be assertive (see scenario 1).

3. Have the first group act out scenario 1. Videotape the scenario. Other groups watch as the scenario is acted out.

4. Review the videotape for all of the retreatants. Discuss with all of the retreatants alternative ways to act in the situation.

5. Have the first group act out scenario 1 using the behaviors decided upon during the discussion. It is important that this be acted out the second time. This reinforces the new behaviors.

6. Have the second group act out scenario 2. Repeat steps 3–5 for each scenario.

7. Summarize the activity. Emphasize that learning how to handle stress in all areas of life prepares us to handle stress that is associated with drug and alcohol abuse.

6:00 p.m. Dinner

One staff person should be available to make announcements and to choose a retreatant to lead the group in prayer before the meal.

7:15 p.m. Panel of recovering young people

Not all of the retreatants have been exposed to the harmful effects of substance abuse. However, all of them will be confronted with the effects eventually. This might be from classmates, friends, or family members. The panel members from AA and NA will share their personal experiences and explain what has worked for them in their recovery. This exposes the retreatants to alternatives in the event they are confronted with a substance-abuse situation.

Staff: one person to introduce the panel members

Materials needed: copies of a counseling referral list that includes meeting times and phone numbers of local chapters of AA, NA, CA, Al-Anon, and Alateen

Description of activities: Introduce the panel and encourage the retreatants to listen attentively. After the panel members have given their presentations, ask for questions from the retreatants. Close the discussion by handing out local listings of meeting times and phone numbers of AA, NA, CA, Al-Anon, and Alateen.

8:45 p.m. Break

9:30 p.m. Reconciliation

Staff: a leader and several priests, depending upon the number of retreatants

Materials needed: a Bible; the song "Change My Heart" from the *Praise 9* album, by Maranatha Music; a tape or record player; and a tape or a record of instrumental music

Description of activities

1. Introduction and prayer: "We have gathered this evening as a Christian community to come before our loving God. Our God offers forgiveness and compassion. We acknowledge that we need help. Jesus, in his deep love, can heal our wounds. Jesus invites us to a change of heart. And so we pray:

"Lord Jesus, compassionate Brother and Savior, we gather this night to celebrate your merciful forgiveness. You call us to change our heart and turn to you. Inspire us by your great love and guide us by your example as we surrender ourselves to you one day at a time. We pray this in your name, Lord Jesus Christ."

2. Reading: Luke 5:27–32 and a reflection on the reading

3. Examination of conscience: First invite the retreatants to reflect on the ways drug and alcohol abuse have influenced their life. Then invite them to reflect upon the following questions:

- Have I been afraid to stick up for what I believe is right?
- Have I been selfish, ignoring the rights and needs of others?
- Have I hurt myself through my own misuse of alcohol and drugs?
- Have I refused to forgive someone who hurt me?
- Have I been honest with myself as well as with others?
- Have I failed to show love and concern for my family?
- Have I failed to pray to God for assistance?
- Have I failed to thank God for gifts received?

4. Song: Lead the retreatants in singing "Change My Heart" (the retreatants learned this song during the morning introduction). If you have arranged for a staff member or a retreatant who is a musician to lead the song, have the musician sing the verses and invite the retreatants to sing the refrain. If a musician is not available, encourage the retreatants to sing along with a recording of the music.

5. Confessions: Introduce the priest (or priests) who will be hearing confessions. Let the retreatants know that if they wish to discuss something in greater depth than time allows, the priest will be available later as well. Dim the lights and play background instrumental music. Suggest that while others are confessing, the time can be used for journal writing, writing a letter to someone, or conversing quietly with other retreatants.

6. Reconciling with one another: Encourage the retreatants to go around the room and converse one-on-one with as many people as possible to offer forgiveness, thanks, or support.

7. Closure: Invite the group to gather in a circle. As a sign of unity, ask everyone to join hands and pray together the Lord's Prayer. Invite them to exchange the sign of peace.

Give a final blessing, such as the following: "May almighty God continue to bless us with forgiveness and courage, in the name of the Father, the Son, and the Holy Spirit. Amen."

11:00 p.m. Break

This break is important because it provides the retreatants with time to unwind before retiring. They have had a full day and will probably need some free time to visit with new friends.

Let the retreatants know the length of the break so they will be prepared to retire after the closedown announcements. If a retreatant has a serious problem and wishes to stay up to discuss it with a retreatant or a staff member, it is *strongly* recommended that a staff member speak briefly with the retreatant and schedule a time tomorrow when they can talk. Both the retreatant and the staff member will be better able to approach the problem when they have had adequate sleep.

Be specific about where the retreatants may go during this break. Consider having snacks with hot and cold drinks available.

11:30 p.m. Closedown

One staff person explains the schedule for the second day and makes announcements. It is advisable to have at least one adult staff member supervise the sleeping areas to assure an orderly closedown.

Retreat Activities: Day 2

7:45 a.m. Wake-up

8:00 a.m. Breakfast

8:45 a.m. Cleanup

One staff person explains the activity. All staff members can help supervise. This time is scheduled to allow the retreatants to change sheets, clean rooms, pack belongings and load the cars or the bus in preparation for departure.

9:30 a.m. Morning prayer

This activity is designed to help the retreatants to appreciate the power of prayer in sustaining the turning of their heart to God in Jesus.

Staff: two people (including one person to assist with handing out paper and pencils)

Materials needed: pencil, paper, and a candle

Description of activities

1. Introduction: "We gather this morning to pray that God's power and love in Jesus will aid us in our efforts to remain steadfast in our change of heart.

"Each of us relates to God in our own way. We choose to pray in ways that are comfortable for us. As a way to encourage you to develop your own style of prayer, this morning you will be given time to create your own prayer for connecting with God."

2. Explanation of the activity: Explain that the retreatants are to create a prayer that connects them with God. Encourage them to be creative. Suggest song, dance, poetry, an essay, an asking theme, a thanking theme, or a praising theme. The retreatants may want to walk around the facility during this time. Explain where they may walk. Pass out paper and pencils.

3. Sharing: After about thirty minutes, call the retreatants back together and form a circle. Invite all to share their prayer. Have a lighted candle for holding while sharing the prayer. Some may not wish to express their prayer aloud because of the personal and possibly confidential nature of the prayer. Let the retreatants know that this is fine. Tell these people to simply pass the candle along in silence. Usually, half of the group is willing to share a prayer.

4. Closure: Pray together the Glory Be.

10:30 a.m. Small group 3: Closure

The retreatants have addressed serious issues, shared personal experiences, and experienced the trust and support of a Christian community. For many of them, this may have been a deeply emotional time. They now need a chance to put closure on their experience. A final review of the retreat activities, and parting gestures of affirmation, can help them return to their home with a positive perspective.

Staff: one person for each small group

Materials needed: none

Description of activities

1. Review: Review the retreat schedule. Invite the retreatants to comment on their feelings as they recall the activities.

2. Goals: Invite the retreatants to state the retreat goals set during small group 1. Ask them to comment on how they did in working toward their goal.

3. Commitments: Encourage the retreatants to talk about resolutions they would like to live out after leaving the retreat.

4. Affirmation: Invite the retreatants to speak to each group member about what they appreciate in that individual. Choose one person to begin. After everyone has had an opportunity to address this person, ask if she or he wishes to make a statement to the group. Do this affirmation for each group member.

5. Summary: Summarize the session and invite each retreatant to make closing comments.

6. Closure: Invite a retreatant to lead the group in a closing prayer.

12:15 p.m. Lunch

One staff person should be available to make announcements, to choose a retreatant to lead the group in prayer before the meal, and to choose retreatants to help with the various parts of the Mass. These include the following:
- reading the first reading: 1 Pet. 5:5–11
- reading the response: "My heart is steadfast, O my God," with Ps. 108:2,3–4,5,6–7
- presenting the offertory gifts
- serving as eucharistic ministers

1:30 p.m. Liturgy

The retreatants carry out those parts of the liturgy for which they are responsible. Invite the retreatants to pray for their personal resolutions during the Prayer of the Faithful. An appropriate gospel reading would be Luke 12:22–31.

2:45 p.m. Wrap-up

Staff: one person (the same person who led the introduction and prayer on day 1)

Materials needed: none

Description of activities: Give a brief presentation using words like the following: "Take a moment to reflect on your current feelings. You have experienced a lot during this retreat. You have been asked to look at a serious subject.

"As you leave the retreat, the choice is yours as to what you will do with all you have learned. I challenge you to take home and put into action any resolutions you made for yourself. Try to integrate into your life what you have learned during the retreat. You prayed, played, practiced coping skills, reconciled yourself with God and others, and shared your experiences with others. Within a Christian community, you asked God to change your heart. I believe God has heard your prayer.

"Remember the power of your prayer to bring God's power and love into your life. Keep your heart open and turned to God by remaining close to Jesus.

"We will pray for you. Please do the same for one another. I invite you to go now to each other and offer a sign of thanks."

Make any necessary announcements.

3:00 p.m. Departure

Part D ▽

A Three-Day Retreat

Chapter 9, "The Lord Is My Shepherd," is a three-day program designed for mature eleventh- and twelfth-grade retreatants. The retreat introduces the participants to the concept and the experience of spiritual direction.

9

The Lord Is My Shepherd: A Spiritual Direction Retreat

"The Lord Is My Shepherd" is a three-day retreat designed for mature eleventh- and twelfth-grade retreatants. The program accommodates ten to twenty people. During the retreat, the participants are introduced to the concept and the experience of spiritual direction.

A growing number of young people are seeking a retreat experience that reaches to a deeper level of their spirituality than the ordinary retreat. Some of these young people have already participated in a number of retreats; others have worked as retreat staff members; still others have never been on a retreat, yet have a strong desire to deepen their relationship with God.

Because this retreat is designed for young people who are looking for more than the ordinary retreat, the participants in this retreat must be carefully screened. They must be stable, inner-directed, prayerful, and open to new experiences. It would be advisable to interview applicants before the retreat.

The main feature of this retreat is the experience of meeting and sharing with a spiritual director. Also, more than the usual amount of quiet time is scheduled. For some of the retreatants, the added quiet time might lead to feelings of loneliness and emptiness, but a balancing measure of sharing in small-group discussions is provided. Handouts are offered for guiding the retreatants during the structured quiet times, but you may want to prepare additional helps for use during the quiet times while others are meeting with spiritual directors and also during the quiet time on the evening of day 2. These helps could include selected scriptural passages with a number of themes, such as commitment, call, covenant, and faithfulness. Also, you may want to prepare some instructions for praying with the Scriptures or nature or music that retreatants could use during their quiet times.

The spiritual director's role is to be a companion to the retreatant during the retreat. The spiritual director prays with the retreatant, affirms the retreatant, confronts gently when necessary, and listens with the heart.

In choosing spiritual directors, keep in mind the importance of their responsibilities. First, the spiritual director must be prayerful. Second, the spiritual director must be comfortable talking to young people. Third, it is recommended that the spiritual director be currently meeting with a spiritual director of his or her own. Arrange for at least one spiritual director for every four retreatants.

Check with local priests or religious educators for suggestions of persons who might be interested in being spiritual directors on this type of retreat. Interview these persons. Make sure they understand adolescent development and have some experience with youth. Explain the role of spiritual director and, together with the spiritual director candidates, decide who best will serve in this way.

Goals

The goals of this retreat are the following:
- That the retreatants meet with spiritual directors
- That the retreatants reflect on God's love and faithfulness in their life
- That the retreatants reflect on their relationship with the Church as the Body of Christ

Schedule

Day 1

6:00 p.m.	Arrival
6:30 p.m.	Dinner
7:45 p.m.	Introduction and prayer
8:30 p.m.	Quiet time and meetings with directors
9:30 p.m.	Break
10:00 p.m.	Evening prayer
11:30 p.m.	Lights out

Day 2

7:45 a.m.	Wake-up
8:00 a.m.	Breakfast
9:15 a.m.	Morning prayer
9:45 a.m.	Quiet time
10:45 a.m.	Small group 1: God
12:00 m.	Lunch
1:00 p.m.	Recreation
2:30 p.m.	Quiet time and meetings with directors
4:30 p.m.	Break
5:00 p.m.	Liturgy
6:00 p.m.	Dinner
7:30 p.m.	Reconciliation
9:00 p.m.	Break
10:00 p.m.	Quiet time
11:30 p.m.	Lights out

Day 3

7:45 a.m.	Wake-up
8:00 a.m.	Breakfast
9:15 a.m.	Morning prayer
9:45 a.m.	Quiet time
10:45 a.m.	Small group 2: Church
12:00 m.	Lunch
1:00 p.m.	Recreation
2:00 p.m.	Quiet time and meetings with directors
4:00 p.m.	Break
4:30 p.m.	Liturgy
5:45 p.m.	Wrap-up
6:00 p.m.	Departure

Materials needed for this retreat: a retreat schedule for each retreatant; blank name tags; materials for a spiritual reading library, such as spiritual reading books, spiritual tapes (musical or verbal); a bibliography of the spiritual library for each retreatant; copies of handouts; a Bible; *Praise and Worship* and *Glory and Praise 2* songbooks; the song "Without Your Love"; a tape or record player; pencils; felt-tip markers; masking tape; butcher paper; and a tape or a record of instrumental music

Items the retreatants should bring: a Bible, a journal, and a pen. Invite those retreatants who play instruments to bring them along.

Retreat Activities: Day 1

6:00 p.m. Arrival

Two staff members welcome and register the retreatants, give them the retreat schedule, help them locate their room, and have them fill out name tags.

6:30 p.m. Dinner

One staff person should be available to make announcements about the evening schedule and to lead the prayer before the meal.

7:45 p.m. Introduction and prayer

Staff: two people (including one to assist with handouts). All staff members need to be present for introductions.

Materials needed: handouts 9–A and 9–B

Description of activities

1. Introduction: Introduce yourself and the staff. Have the retreatants introduce themselves to the group by giving their name and why they have come to the retreat.

Introduce the theme of the retreat by saying something like the following: "As followers of Jesus, we are called to be a community of faith and love. Throughout our life, we travel together to God. Historically, seekers of God have chosen spiritual companions to accompany them in seeking God's way. Perhaps you have known someone who has been a spiritual companion to you.

"In Ezekiel [34:11–16] God speaks to us saying 'I myself will look after and tend my sheep. . . . The lost I will seek out, the strayed I will bring back, the injured I will bind up, the sick I will heal.' This image of the caring shepherd is used throughout the Scriptures. The greatest spiritual companion we could have to walk with us is the Good Shepherd.

"To remind each of you of the spiritual companionship offered to us by God, we have chosen 'The Lord Is My Shepherd' as the theme for this retreat. During this retreat, I pray that you will become more open to the promptings of God in your life.

"There will be a number of new experiences for you during this retreat. Each of you has been assigned a spiritual director. This person will be a spiritual companion who will accompany you on your journey to God during these three days of retreat. You and your spiritual director will meet each day.

"Another important part of this retreat is the more than usual amount of quiet time that has been scheduled. In silence, God speaks to our heart. Usually, we have so many distractions that we never find the time or the place to quietly place ourselves in the presence of God. You will have that quiet time available to you during the retreat.

"The quiet times may be difficult for you. You might feel uncomfortable, empty, and lonely. If this happens, stay with the feelings and consciously place yourself in the arms of the Good Shepherd. When you meet with your director, talk about these feelings. The two of you can then decide what is best for you.

"During the retreat, you will be asked to write in a journal, listen to music, or read. We have a spiritual library available. Your spiritual director will have a bibliography listing the tapes and books that are available in this library.

2. *Prayer:* Distribute handout 9-A, "Psalm 23." Invite the retreat community to join in praying together the psalm on the handout.

3. *Orientation:* Explain the guidelines for using the facility. Using the chart on handout 9-B, "Spiritual Director Meetings," assign spiritual directors. Explain where and when the directors will meet the retreatants. Explain that while the spiritual director is meeting with individual retreatants, other retreatants can use the time to reflect on a retreat goal, write in their journal, pray, or go for a walk.

8:30 p.m. Quiet time and meetings with directors

This is meant to be an introductory meeting. Each retreatant will meet her or his spiritual director for fifteen minutes. Some retreatants will be ready and willing to talk a lot. Others will not know what to say.

Staff: at least one spiritual director for every four retreatants

Materials needed: spiritual library bibliography

Description of activities: The spiritual director and the retreatant introduce themselves to each other and pray for God's blessing on the retreat.

The spiritual director explains her or his role with the retreatant, using words like the following: "A spiritual director is a companion to a retreatant during the retreat. A spiritual director is *not* a guide. A guide knows the way. I do not know the way God is leading you, but I can assist you to find a means to grow in a relationship with God. Throughout the retreat, we will be working together as a team."

Discuss the retreatant's personal life concerns and related goal for the retreat and review the bibliography of spiritual library resources.

The spiritual director offers a closing prayer.

9:30 p.m. Break

During this break, one staff member chooses a retreatant to read the scriptural passage during the evening prayer.

10:00 p.m. Evening prayer

This is a simple prayer service in which the retreatants call upon God to walk with them during the retreat. Because many of the young people are experienced retreatants, allow adequate time for their prayers. The evening prayer also provides a closure for the day.

Staff: two people (including one to assist with handing out songbooks)

Materials needed: a Bible and *Praise and Worship* songbooks

Description of activities

1. *Introduction:* "Tonight we gather to place ourselves in the hands of the Good Shepherd. Before we retire, let us reflect on how God has always been faithful and loving to us."

2. *Reading:* Ps. 139:1–6,13–18. Pause between verses 6 and 13.

3. *Goals:* Invite the retreatants to recall the personal retreat goal they discussed with their spiritual director during the introductory meeting and to offer a prayer asking God to assist them in working toward this goal.

4. *Song:* Invite the retreatants to join in singing "The Lord Is My Shepherd" in the *Praise and Worship* songbook.

5. *Closure:* Invite the retreatants to retire to their room reflecting upon God's love and faithfulness shown to them throughout their life. Encourage them to fall asleep with this thought in their mind.

11:30 p.m. Lights out

Retreat Activities: Day 2

7:45 a.m. Wake-up

8:00 a.m. Breakfast

A staff member chooses a retreatant to lead the

prayer before the meal and to read the scriptural passage during the morning prayer.

9:15 a.m. Morning prayer

The leader introduces the activity and invites the retreatants to prayerfully reflect on the way God intervenes in their life. The morning prayer sets the tone for the day. Last night the retreatants retired reflecting upon God's faithfulness to them. This morning's prayer centers around remembering God's interventions in their life.

Staff: two people (including one to assist with the handouts)

Materials needed: handout 9-C; a Bible; a tape or record of "Without Your Love" from the album *Best Bits,* by Roger Daltrey; journals; pencils; and a tape or record player

Description of activities

1. Introduction: Distribute handout 9-C, "Blessing Prayer." Then say something like the following: "Good morning! Last night you retired reflecting upon the many ways that God has shown love and faithfulness throughout your life. Later this morning we will share our own stories of God's faithfulness with each other in small-group discussions. Before we do that, though, let's begin our day by remembering that we are in the holy presence of God." Pause.

2. Reading: Ps. 139:7–12. Pause. Following the reading, play the song "Without Your Love" from the album *Best Bits,* by Roger Daltrey.

3. Closure: Invite the retreatants to offer individual prayers. Then join together in praying the "Blessing Prayer" on handout 9-C.

9:45 a.m. Quiet time

Staff: one person to explain the activity and distribute handouts

Materials needed: pencils and handout 9-D

Description of activities: Distribute handout 9-D, "Reflection Questions for Day 2 Quiet Time." Encourage the retreatants to write in their journal during the quiet time. Pass out pencils if needed. Assign small groups and explain where the groups will be meeting after the quiet time.

This is a time for quiet reflection on the questions from the quiet-time handout. Encourage the retreatants to write their reflections in their journal. After the quiet time, the retreatants should go directly to the small-group meeting areas.

10:45 a.m. Small group 1: God

Because the retreatants have already had the quiet time to write their reflections, they will come into this group well prepared and ready to begin.

Staff: one person to lead each small group

Materials needed: a felt-tip marker, butcher paper, masking tape, and handout 9-D

Description of activities

1. Introductions: Invite each person to introduce himself or herself to the group.

2. Guidelines: Help the retreatants establish discussion guidelines and post them for all to see (see page 41).

3. Discussion: Encourage the retreatants to participate in a discussion of the questions on handout 9-D, "Reflection Questions for Day 2 Quiet Time." Begin by asking if anyone is willing to share with the group what they wrote in their journal. Have them identify the question for the response they are sharing. This will keep the discussion moving and help others to plug into the discussion. As the leader, take an active role in this discussion only if necessary. Most of the retreatants will have the experience and the skills to keep the discussion going.

4. Summary: Summarize the discussion. Invite each person to make a closing comment.

5. Closure: Invite a retreatant to offer a closing prayer.

12:00 m. Lunch

One staff person should be available to make announcements and to choose a retreatant to lead the prayer before the meal.

1:00 p.m. Recreation

This recreational period is unstructured. Have recreational equipment available and encourage the retreatants to go outside for some type of exercise.

2:30 p.m. Quiet time and meetings with directors

This is a time for each retreatant and her or his spiritual director to meet and review how the retreat is going. The meetings are thirty minutes.

While the directors are meeting with individual retreatants, other retreatants can use the time to review their retreat goal, to record thoughts and feelings about the various activities in their journal, to pray, or to use the spiritual library.

Staff: at least one spiritual director for every four retreatants

Materials needed: handout 9-D

Description of activities: The spiritual director and the retreatant prayerfully recall they are in the presence of God. The spiritual director reviews the retreat schedule and invites the retreatant to discuss her or his feelings and thoughts during the activities. The retreatant may have recorded these in a journal. Handout 9-D, "Reflection Questions for Day 2 Quiet Time," which was distributed during the morning quiet time, may be useful here.

Close with a prayer.

4:30 p.m. Break

During the break a staff person chooses retreatants to assist with the following liturgical responsibilities:
- reading the first reading: Isa. 40:9–11
- reading the response: "Praise the name of the Lord," with Ps. 113:1–5
- presenting the offertory gifts
- serving as eucharistic ministers

5:00 p.m. Liturgy

Individuals carry out those parts of the Mass for which they are responsible. An appropriate gospel reading is John 1:14–18.

6:00 p.m. Dinner

One staff person should be available to make announcements and to choose a retreatant to lead the prayer before the meal.

7:30 p.m. Reconciliation

Staff: a leader and several priests, depending upon the number of retreatants.

Materials needed: a Bible, a tape or record player, and a tape or a record of instrumental music

Description of activities

1. Introduction and prayer: "We have gathered this evening as a Christian community. Throughout the day we have examined ways God intervenes in our life. We have reflected on the great love and faithfulness God has shown to each of us.

"As we strive to be a community of faith and love, we realize that we fall short of our goal. Because we do fall short, it is important that we take the time on a regular basis to renew our relationships with God and one another by asking forgiveness.

"Tonight, we have gathered in a spirit of reconciliation. We place ourselves before God, remembering the love and faithfulness that we have known throughout our life."

2. Reading: John 10:1–5

3. Homily

4. Examination of conscience: Lead the retreatants through an examination of conscience, using the following questions. Read the questions slowly.
- Does my behavior reflect Christian values?
- Do I take sufficient time each day to deepen my relationship with God?
- Am I sensitive to the needs of the people around me?
- Do I speak honestly even when it is difficult?
- Do I take sufficient time to strengthen my relationships with my family members?
- Do I forgive others who have hurt me?
- Are there other areas in my life where my thoughts, words, and actions have not reflected Christian values?

5. Confessions: Indicate to the retreatants the priest (or priests) who will be hearing confessions. Let them know that if they wish to discuss something in greater depth than time allows, the priest will be available later as well. Dim the lights and play background instrumental music. Suggest that while others are confessing, they use the time to reflect, write in a journal, write a letter to someone they care for, read from the Scriptures, and the like.

6. Closure: Invite the retreatants to join in a common penance by praying a prayer of trust, for example Psalm 23, which was used in the beginning of the retreat (see handout 9-A). End with a blessing prayer, for example, "May God continue to bless you with presence as a Good Shepherd, leading you to new life and new spirit. We ask this in Jesus' name. Amen."

9:00 p.m. Break

During this break, have snacks available for the retreatants.

10:00 p.m. Quiet time

11:30 p.m. Lights out

Retreat Activities: Day 3

7:45 a.m. Wake-up

8:00 a.m. Breakfast

During this time, a staff member chooses a retreatant to lead the prayer before the meal and to read the scriptural passage during the morning prayer.

9:15 a.m. Morning prayer

So far, the retreatants have examined ways that God has touched their life. This prayer sets the tone for the day by providing time to reflect on Mary's choice to give her life for the Body of Christ.

Staff: one person

Materials needed: a Bible and *Glory and Praise 2* songbooks

Description of activities

1. Introduction: "Yesterday you reflected on and discussed God's love and faithfulness. Last night we came together to reconcile ourselves to God and to each other. This morning I invite you to think about the call each one of us has to build up the Body of Christ. Mary, the Mother of Jesus, is a great example of the selflessness involved in building up the Body of Christ.

"To begin this prayer service, we will listen to a reading from Saint Luke's Gospel. This reading is Mary's response to her cousin Elizabeth after Mary had consented to God's will that she become the mother of Jesus. Mary is an example of a person who allowed her life to be changed drastically. Her willingness to give of herself led to the birth of our Savior and Lord, Jesus Christ. Mary is our example of the selfless giving that is needed in order to build up the Body of Christ."

2. Reading: Luke 1:46–55. Pause.

3. Song: Invite the retreatants to sing "My Soul Rejoices" in *Glory and Praise 2*.

9:45 a.m. Quiet time

Staff: two people (including one person to help with the handouts)

Materials needed: journals, pencils, and handout 9–E

Description of activities: Distribute handout 9–E, "Reflection Questions for Day 3 Quiet Time." Encourage the retreatants to quietly reflect on the questions on the handout and to write in their journal. Remind the retreatants that the small groups will meet immediately following the quiet time.

10:45 a.m. Small group 2: Church

This discussion on the Church calls for delicate and sensitive facilitation. The retreatants may be at various levels of relationship with the Church. For some young people, the institutional Church still represents authority, so they may strongly resist becoming an active member in the Church. For others, the members of the body of the Church do not live up to idealistic expectations. Still others may have a positive perspective on the Church, both as an institution and as a body of people.

Staff: one person to lead each small group

Materials needed: handout 9–E

Description of activities

1. Guidelines: Review the discussion guidelines, especially stressing the importance of confidentiality.

2. Discussion: Encourage the retreatants to participate in a discussion of the questions on handout 9–E, "Reflection Questions for Day 3 Quiet Time." Begin by focusing on the first question, "What does *church* mean for you?" Then move to the other questions on the handout. During this discussion, encourage the retreatants to share not only their beliefs but also the experiences that have influenced them in formulating these beliefs.

As the leader, take an active role in this discussion only if necessary. Most of the retreatants will have the experience and the skills necessary to keep the discussion going.

3. Summary: Summarize the discussion. Invite each person to make a closing comment.

4. Closure: Invite a retreatant to offer a closing prayer.

12:00 m. Lunch

One staff person should be available to make announcements and to choose a retreatant to lead the prayer before the meal.

1:00 p.m. Recreation

If necessary, the retreatants can use this time to clean up their room and pack their belongings.

2:00 p.m. Quiet time and meetings with directors

This meeting is designed to help the retreatants put closure on the retreat experience. Each retreatant will meet his or her spiritual director for thirty minutes.

While the directors are meeting with individual retreatants, other retreatants can use the time to review thoughts and feelings recorded in their journal, to reflect on resolutions or new commitments, to pray, or to use the spiritual library.

Staff: at least one spiritual director for every four retreatants

Materials needed: the retreatants' journals and handout 9-E

Description of activities: The spiritual director and the retreatant prayerfully recall they are in the presence of God. The spiritual director invites the retreatant to discuss any journal entries made during the retreat. Then they discuss resolutions or commitments made as a result of the retreat experience. Handout 9-E, "Reflection Questions for Day 3 Quiet Time," which was distributed during the morning quiet time, may be useful here.

To close, the spiritual director invites the retreatant to offer a prayer.

4:00 p.m. Break

During this break, a staff member chooses retreatants to assist with the following liturgical responsibilities:
- reading the first reading: Ezek. 34:11–16
- reading the response, "The Lord is my shepherd, I shall not want," with Ps. 23:2–6
- presenting the offertory gifts
- serving as eucharistic ministers

4:30 p.m. Liturgy

Distribute handout 9-F, "Communion Meditation." Retreatants carry out those parts of the liturgy for which they are responsible. John 10:11–18 is an appropriate gospel reading, and you may include the communion meditation on handout 9-F.

5:45 p.m. Wrap-up

Staff: one person

Materials needed: none

Description of activities: "During this retreat, you have had a lot of time to reflect upon your relationship with God and others. You have had a spiritual companion to walk with you. You also have had time to reflect on the companionship that the Good Shepherd offers to you each day of your life.

"As you prepare to return home, I urge you to make every effort to be faithful to the resolutions or commitments you made to yourself. Pray daily for the grace to deepen your relationship with God . . . the Good Shepherd.

"As a way to help you prepare to leave the retreat, I would like to read a passage from *Wellsprings*, by Anthony de Mello." (*Note:* You might also consider making this passage into a prayer card to be given to the retreatants as a memento of the retreat.)

"My retreat has come to an end,
and I think of the days that I have spent
in these surroundings.

I see an image of myself as I was when I came here
and I look at myself as I am today
at the close of the retreat.

I think of the persons and places
that have been a part of my retreat.
To each of them I speak in gratitude
and to each I say goodbye:
other places, other persons call to me
and I must go.

I think of the experiences I have had,
the graces I have been granted
in this place.
For each of these too I am grateful.

I think of the kind of life I have lived here,
the atmosphere, the daily schedule,
I say goodbye to them:
another type of life awaits me,
other graces, other experiences.

And as I say goodbye to persons,
places,
things,
events,
experiences,
and graces,
I do so under life's imperious bidding:
if I wish to be alive
I must learn to die at every moment,
that is, to say goodbye, let go, move on.

When this is done, I turn to face the future
and I say, "Welcome."

. . . .

I think of the work that waits for me,
the people I shall meet,
the type of life I shall be living,
the events that will take place tomorrow.
And I extend my arms in welcome
to the summons of the future.

(Pp. 148–149)

Invite the retreatants to offer to one another a sign of thanks.

6:00 p.m. Departure

Scriptural Prayer: Psalm 23

Right: Yahweh, you are my shepherd;
I shall not want.
In verdant pastures you give me repose.

Left: Beside restful waters you lead me;
you refresh my soul.
You guide me in right paths
for your name's sake.

Right: Even though I walk in the dark valley
I fear no evil;
for you are at my side.
Your rod and your staff give me courage.

Left: You spread the table before me
in the sight of my foes.
You anoint my head with oil;
my cup brims over.

All: Only goodness and kindness follow me
all the days of my life;
and I shall dwell in your house
for years to come.

Meetings with Spiritual Directors

Assign each retreatant to a spiritual director (SD) for the three meeting times listed using the chart. Write retreatants' initials in the space provided.

	SD1	SD2	SD3	SD4	SD5
Day 1 (15 min.) 8:30 p.m.					
8:45 p.m.					
9:00 p.m.					
9:15 p.m.					
Day 2 (30 min.) 2:30 p.m.					
3:00 p.m.					
3:30 p.m.					
4:00 p.m.					
Day 3 (30 min.) 2:00 p.m.					
2:30 p.m.					
3:00 p.m.					
3:30 p.m.					

Blessing Prayer

Lord God, we bless You
    and are filled with gratitude for the numerous gifts,
    the countless blessings,
    that come to us from You.
Your blessings come in times of joy,
    in times of victory, in success and honor,
    and they come as well in times of pain and sorrow,
    in sickness and defeat.
Your blessings, however, come always as *life.*

We take pleasure in the fruit of Your creation,
    in the earthen blessings
    of fish and bird, tree and flower,
    each the harvest of Your divine heart.

We take delight in our eyes,
    in our ears, arms and legs.
We find joy in holidays and vacations,
    and in our work as well.
We thank You, Lord of Gifts,
    for friendships, family and fun.
In winning and in losing—
    in being last as well as first—
    we take relish in the challenge and adventure
    of Your great gift of life.
Lord, we thank You for all the gifts
    that flow fully, day and night,
    into our lives.

Today, with full hearts,
    in the company of Jesus, Mary,
    and of all Your Saints,
    we bless You for all the good that has come to us.

Blessed are You, Lord our God,
    who in the richness of Your divine love,
    blesses us with good things.
Amen.

        (Hays, *Prayers for the Domestic Church,* p. 51)

Reflection Questions for Day 2 Quiet Time

**Where can I go from your spirit? . . .
If I go up to the heavens,
you are there.
(Psalm 139:7–8)**

Please read the following questions and write your reflections in your journal.

1. What is your image of God?
2. What do you want in your relationship with God?
3. Are you satisfied with your present relationship with God?
4. What would be the ideal relationship with God? How could you achieve this?
5. What do you want from your life?

Reflection Questions for Day 3 Quiet Time

Mary proclaimed the greatness of the Lord in her Magnificat found in Luke's Gospel (1:46–55). She also expressed the joy that she felt in experiencing the love of her Savior.

As we grow in our relationship with God and with each other, let us reflect on the following scriptural passage:

> **Let us profess the truth in love and grow to the full maturity of Christ the head. Through him the whole body grows, and with the proper functioning of the members joined firmly together each supporting ligament, builds itself up in love. (Ephesians 4:15–16)**

Please read the following questions and write your reflections in your journal.

1. What does *church* mean for you?
2. What is your attitude toward the Church?
3. What is your attitude toward worship?
4. What do you need to do to participate more fully in the life of the Church?
5. What would be your ideal church community? How can you achieve that dream?
6. What does your baptismal commitment mean to you?
7. What is your sacramental experience?
8. As a result of this retreat experience, what commitments or resolutions would you like to make?

Communion Meditation

Lord God, You who know the secrets of our hearts,
    come now and fill me with the spirit of sincerity
    as I pledge myself to You
    and to the coming of Your kingdom.

Lord, I desire to serve You with all my heart,
    with all my soul and with all my strength.
I surrender myself to Your holy plan for me
    as I seek to be perfect as You are perfect.

. . . .

May I strive to live within the spirit of holy poverty,
    living a simple way of life.
May my greatest possession be Your love
    and the love of those around me.
I strive for excellence in loving,
    asking that my love be always chaste and whole.
May I strive to be obedient and open
    to the mystery of Your voice within me,
    willing to embrace whatever You may ask of me.

Lord and Friend
    I rededicate myself
    to a life of prayer and worship of You.
May a song of praise be the constant melody of my heart.
I re-commit myself
    to serve the needs of those around me
    and the needs of all the world.
May I find my salvation *here*
    at this time and in this place where I now live.
May my union with those who share my commitment
    be a source of confirmation and inspiration to me.

Lord, I marvel that You, in Your divine wisdom,
    have chosen me to be an instrument
    of Your creative salvation.
May all the work of my hands,
    even my failings and stumblings,
    be leaven to make that much desired Kingdom a reality.
Bless me now with Your abounding love
    as I promise to be Your friend, servant and holy minister.
May I ever live out this commitment,
    in Your Name: Father, Son and Holy Spirit.
Amen.

(Hays, *Prayers for the Domestic Church,* p. 44)

Part E ▽

A Four-Day Retreat

Chapter 10, "Standing on Holy Ground," is a four-day camping retreat designed for high-school-aged persons. During this retreat, the participants have the opportunity to experience God through the beauty of creation as seen in the natural gifts of the outdoors, such as mountains, lakes, trees, and rivers.

10

Standing on Holy Ground: A Camping Retreat

"Standing on Holy Ground" is a four-day camping retreat designed for high-school-aged retreatants. This retreat is loosely structured because the focus is to enjoy the beauty of nature and to rest in the gifts of creation.

An outdoor retreat takes the individual out of the everyday environment in order to gain perspective. An opportunity like this is especially helpful to young people, who are so busy with school, family, and work commitments that they seldom have time to stop and enjoy the beauty of creation. Praise of God comes easily in natural surroundings.

An outdoor retreat also gives retreatants the chance to set aside the nonessentials. Getting back to nature has a healing and renewing effect. It is hoped staff and retreatants will return renewed, refreshed, and more able to see God in all that surrounds them.

National, state, and county parks throughout the United States offer group campsites. A group site, rather than individual sites, offers the advantages of a larger area for tents and a number of tables that can be moved together. Most of these sites need to be reserved two months ahead of the retreat date, especially if the retreat is in the summer. When choosing a site for the retreat, look for parks that offer a variety of trails for hiking, because the retreat includes two five-mile hikes. Another option would be to plan a retreat that includes a canoe or a raft trip. Make sure a staff member is familiar with the trails or the water route before taking the retreatants on them.

In any camping, hiking, or canoeing outing, a certain amount of risk is involved. Parents as well as retreatants must be reminded of this. Certainly, participating in an outdoor retreat offers the beauty of the natural surroundings, and most often the trip is worth the minimal risks. Leaders and retreatants should consistently make choices that keep risks at a minimum. This includes traveling in pairs when leaving the campsite; knowing of emergency services in the vicinity; using a compass, maps, and trail guides, and being cautious when swimming in creeks, rivers, or lakes. Serious injuries can occur when diving into unfamiliar water.

Do not fill the schedule with extra activities. The outdoors offers a lot to explore. Encourage journal writing and taking quiet time alone or with others.

Depending on the location of the campsite and the time of the year, rearrange the schedule in order to make the most of daylight. Check the sunrise and sunset times as you plan the retreat. Revise times for meals so that cleanup takes place during daylight hours.

This program has the potential to offer a wonderful experience for the retreatants and the staff. Conscientious planning will help make the retreat a success.

Goals

The goals of this retreat are the following:
- That the retreatants build community by working together in camp, preparing meals, and hiking
- That the retreatants experience God through the beauty of creation in natural gifts, such as mountains, lakes, trees, and rivers
- That the retreatants experience God through an expression of love from their parents, communicated through letters

A Camping Retreat ▽ 91

Schedule

Day 1

3:00 p.m.	Arrival and camp setup
4:00 p.m.	Introduction and prayer
5:00 p.m.	Dinner preparation
6:00 p.m.	Dinner
7:00 p.m.	Cleanup
7:30 p.m.	Liturgy
9:00 p.m.	Campfire
11:00 p.m.	Closedown

Day 2

7:30 a.m.	Wake-up
8:00 a.m.	Breakfast
9:00 a.m.	Morning prayer
9:30 a.m.	Pack for hike
10:00 a.m.	Hike 1
12:30 p.m.	Lunch and recreation
2:00 p.m.	Hike 1 (return to camp)
5:00 p.m.	Dinner preparation
6:00 p.m.	Dinner
7:15 p.m.	Skits and discussion: Parent-teen relationships
10:00 p.m.	Campfire
11:00 p.m.	Closedown

Day 3

7:30 a.m.	Wake-up
8:00 a.m.	Breakfast
9:00 a.m.	Morning prayer
9:30 a.m.	Pack for hike
10:00 a.m.	Hike 2
12:30 p.m.	Lunch and recreation
2:00 p.m.	Hike 2 (return to camp)
5:00 p.m.	Dinner preparation
6:00 p.m.	Dinner
7:30 p.m.	Evening prayer
7:45 p.m.	Affirmation
10:30 p.m.	Campfire
11:00 p.m.	Closedown

Day 4

7:30 a.m.	Wake-up
8:00 a.m.	Breakfast
9:00 a.m.	Cleanup
10:00 a.m.	Liturgy
11:00 a.m.	Departure

Before the retreat: Write to the parents or the guardians of the retreatants, asking them to write a letter of affirmation to their son or daughter. Remind them that this is to be a surprise for the retreatants (see sample 10–A, "Letter to Parents"). Include the permission and medical-release form (see handout 2–A) along with the letter. This is especially important for a retreat such as this one. Bring the letters and release forms on the retreat.

Make arrangements with a priest to celebrate the eucharistic liturgies on days 1 and 4.

Using the registration list, form the retreatants into teams for camp duties during the retreat (see handout 10–B, "Meal Duties," for an assignment roster).

Prepare menus (see foods suggested below).

Materials needed for this retreat

Camping equipment: tents and tent stakes, canvas or ground cloths, a portable radio, a hatchet, matches, flashlights and spare batteries, a lantern and fuel, a camp stove and fuel, cooking utensils, a griddle, pots and pans, plates, cups, tableware, a coffeepot, a can opener, a large pot, water containers, an ice chest, biodegradable soap, a washing bowl, rope, trash bags, dishcloths, potholders, a pot scrubber, napkins, paper towels, aluminum foil, a plastic table cover, insect repellent, a snakebite kit, a first-aid kit, maps, a compass, and a whistle

Food: Suggested foods are dried soups, meat (canned, fresh, or frozen), fruits and vegetables (canned, fresh, or frozen), milk, fruit juices, cocoa, tea, coffee, breads, cereals, pancake mix and syrup, bacon and eggs, butter or margarine, sugar, salt, pepper, mustard, catsup, mayonnaise, cookies, cooking oil, and marshmallows, crackers, and chocolate bars for s'mores

Items the retreatants should bring: a canteen, a Bible, a journal, a pen, a tent and a pad, toiletries, towels, a sleeping bag and a pillow, medications, comfortable shoes, a flashlight, a swimsuit, a day pack, sunglasses, rain gear, clothes for high and low temperatures, sunscreen, and a musical instrument (if they play one and would like to accompany the singing)

Miscellaneous: copies of handouts and the songs "Spirit of God" and "Holy Ground"

Retreat Activities: Day 1

Before leaving for the campsite, gather everyone together to pray for a safe journey. Use words such as the following:

Blessed are You, Lord our God,
> for You have created a wide and wonderful world
> in which we can travel.

We ask Your blessing upon us
> as we are about to leave on a journey.

Be our ever-near companion . . .
> and spread the road before us
> with beauty and adventure.

May all the highways ahead of us
> be free of harm and evil.

. . . .

On this trip may we take with us
> as part of our traveling equipment
> a heart wrapped in wonder with which to rejoice
> in all that we . . . meet.

Along with the clothing of wonder,
> may we have room in our luggage
> for a mystic map
> by which we can find the invisible meanings
> of the events of this journey—
> of possible disappointments and delays,
> of possible breakdowns and rainy day troubles.

Always awake to Your Sacred Presence
> and to Your . . . compassionate love,
> may we see in all that happens to us,
> in the beautiful and the bad,
> the mystery of Your holy plan.

May the blessing of Your name, Father, Son and Holy Spirit,
> be upon us throughout this trip,
> and bring us home again in safety and peace.

(Hays, *Prayers for the Domestic Church*, p. 35)

3:00 p.m. Arrival and camp setup

Unload the bus or the cars, arrange the tables, set up the tents, and place the food in storage lockers. Have the retreatants stay near the campsite until guidelines are reviewed during the next activity.

4:00 p.m. Introduction and prayer

The introduction sets the tone for the retreat. It can be easy for the retreatants to forget the purpose of the outing.

Staff: two people. All staff members need to be present for the introductions.

Materials needed: journals, pens, and handouts 10-A and 10-B

Description of activities

1. Introduction: Introduce yourself and the staff to the retreatants and ask the retreatants to introduce themselves to the group by giving their name and what they hope to gain from the retreat.

Introduce the theme of the retreat by saying something like the following: "There is a story in the Jewish Scriptures, or Old Testament [Exodus 3:1–10], that tells of when an angel of the Lord appeared to Moses in fire flaming out of a bush. Moses moved closer to see why the fire was not consuming the bush. As Moses moved closer, God called to him and told him to remove his sandals because he was standing on holy ground.

"We too are standing on holy ground. 'Standing on Holy Ground' is the theme of our camping retreat. Often we forget to notice the sacredness and the beauty of creation. By coming away from our ordinary environment for this retreat, we had to leave behind the nonessentials. In leaving these behind, we will have the opportunity to open all of our senses to the works of God in nature around us. Smell the fresh air, listen to the sounds of nature during the day and at night, touch the land, and carefully examine your surroundings.

"This is holy ground. We have gathered in God's name. God is manifested to us in the beauty of nature and through one another. Keep this in mind during the retreat. Listen to God speak to you. Open your ears to God's Word. Celebrate God's love as a Christian community.

"Throughout the retreat, we will refer to a number of scriptural passages. Write these passages down in your journal. During free time, look up these passages and prayerfully reflect on them. Write in your journal any thoughts and feelings that come to you."

2. Prayer: Lead the retreat community in prayer. You may use handout 10-A, "Blessed Are You, Lord Our God, for Silence and Solitude."

3. Guidelines: Explain the guidelines for the campsite. Refer to any information provided by the park service when reservations were made. Include the following guidelines:

- When leaving the campsite, inform an adult about your destination and time of return.
- Travel in pairs.
- Stay on trails.
- Pack out what you pack in (do not litter).
- Keep food in storage lockers (do not feed animals).
- Be cautious around unfamiliar lakes, rivers, or creeks. Swimming and diving accidents are a result of misuse.

4. Meal duties: The retreatants have already been formed into teams. Assign meal duties using handout 10–B. The teams include an adult and two or three retreatants. Explain where the list of duties will be posted.

5:00 p.m. Dinner preparation

Team 1 prepares dinner. Other retreatants can use this time to explore or relax. Some retreatants might gather firewood, if this is permitted by the park. Remind the retreatants of the safety guidelines mentioned earlier.

6:00 p.m. Dinner

One staff person should be available to make announcements and to choose a retreatant to lead the group in a prayer before the meal.

7:00 p.m. Cleanup

Team 2 cleans up after the meal. During this time, staff members choose retreatants for duties during the liturgy. Below is a list of responsibilities:
- reading the first reading: Exod. 34:4–6,8–9
- reading the response: "The heavens declare the glory of God," with Psalm 19
- presenting the offertory gifts
- serving as eucharistic ministers

7:30 p.m. Liturgy

The purpose of having a liturgy at the beginning of the retreat is to help the retreatants feel the sacredness of the natural surroundings. They worship together as a community and are reminded of God's presence in others as well as in nature.

Check the time for sunset and schedule the liturgy so that there is adequate light. If this is not possible, use candles or lanterns.

During the Prayer of the Faithful, invite the retreatants to offer a prayer that includes their personal goal for the retreat.

The following gospel reading and meditation song are suggested:
- gospel reading: John 12:44–50
- communion meditation: "Holy Ground" from the album *Be Exalted*, by John Michael Talbot, or "Holy Ground" from the album *Read the Book, Don't Wait for the Movie,* by Whiteheart

9:00 p.m. Campfire

Community can be built by singing camp songs or telling camp stories. This time is scheduled for the retreatants to unwind in a lighthearted atmosphere. The leader of this activity encourages the retreatants to gather around the campfire and invites them to tell any camp stories they might know.

If a musician (retreatant or staff member) is available, he or she can lead retreatants in singing familiar songs. Songbooks or handouts are not necessary for this activity. Having limited resources challenges the retreatants to be more creative. If no one wants to sing or tell camp stories, encourage the retreatants to sit around the campfire talking to one another. End the evening by again singing "Holy Ground."

11:00 p.m. Closedown

One staff member explains the schedule for the next day and makes any other announcements.

Retreat Activities: Day 2

7:30 a.m. Wake-up

8:00 a.m. Breakfast

Team 3 prepares the meal. One staff person should be available to make announcements and to choose a retreatant to lead the group in prayer before the meal.

Team 4 cleans up after the meal. During cleanup, team 5 prepares the lunch that will be taken on the hike.

9:00 a.m. Morning prayer

During day 2, the retreatants take time to notice the works of God in nature. The morning prayer sets the focus for the day.

Staff: one person

Materials needed: Bibles, pens, journals

Description of activities: Explain that the purpose of the morning prayer is to reflect silently and prayerfully upon the works of God in nature. Invite the retreatants to read Sir. 42:15–43:35.

Encourage the retreatants to walk around the area noticing the beauty of nature. Remind them to write in their journals any reflections or inspirations they might have. (Allow twenty minutes for this.)

Gather the retreatants and invite them to offer observations or prayers of praise. Close by praying the Glory Be.

9:30 a.m. Pack for hike

Make sure adequate supplies are packed. These include water (at least one quart per person), clothing, a compass, maps, a trail guide, a first-aid kit, sunglasses, swimwear, sunscreen, trash bags, and lunch. Persons who have asthma, diabetes, or other medical concerns need to be reminded to bring along medication or food as deemed necessary.

Review the camping guidelines given at the beginning of the retreat.

10:00 a.m. Hike 1

During this hike, encourage the retreatants to explore the works of God as found in the natural surroundings.

An adult staff member should be familiar with the trail chosen for the hike. Teenaged retreatants can hike an average of two miles per hour. At higher elevations (seven thousand to nine thousand feet), breathing can be difficult. Keep this in mind when planning the trip.

During the hike, encourage the hikers to look out for one another. Place the slower hikers in front of the group in order to keep the group together. Plan the hike so the group reaches a suitable area for eating lunch, such as a creek, a stream, or a lake.

12:30 p.m. Lunch and recreation

One staff person should be available to make announcements and to choose a retreatant to lead the group in a prayer before the meal. Be sure to carry back any trash.

2:00 p.m. Hike 1 (return to camp)

The hike back is a good time for the staff members to talk with retreatants individually about the retreat goal stated during the Prayer of the Faithful at the evening liturgy on day 1.

5:00 p.m. Dinner preparation

Team 6 prepares the meal. Other retreatants can use this time to explore or relax. Some retreatants might gather firewood. Remind the retreatants of the safety guidelines mentioned earlier.

6:00 p.m. Dinner

One staff person should be available to make announcements and to choose a retreatant to lead the group in a prayer before the meal. Team 7 cleans up after the meal.

7:15 p.m. Skits and discussion: Parent-teen relationships

The first part of this activity, performing skits, is designed to be playful. At the same time, it can help the retreatants reflect on relationships with parents. Later, the affirmation letters from the retreatants' parents are distributed.

Be aware of the time of sunset before beginning this activity and plan accordingly, as the retreatants will need adequate light to read their letter.

Staff: four persons (including three people to assist in passing out the letters from parents)

Materials needed: the letters from the retreatants' parents

Description of activities

1. Skits: Divide the retreatants into four teams and assign skits. The retreatants are to decide upon the specifics of the skit (names, ages, family setting, context, etc.).
- team 1: parents are upset over their son's report card
- team 2: parents explain to their daughter that she will attend Sunday Mass with the family
- team 3: son wants to go to a pizza party but has not finished the chores he promised he would do
- team 4: daughter comes home two hours after curfew

When they are ready, invite the teams to perform the skits.

2. Discussion: Facilitate a discussion about parent-teen relationships. If the group is larger than twenty, divide the retreatants into small groups. Begin with the following questions and then encourage retreatants to talk about their relationship(s) with their parent(s). Remind the retreatants about the importance of confidentiality.
- Have you experienced any of the situations portrayed in the skits?
- If so, what were your feelings at the time?
- What did you do? What would you do differently now?
- What is difficult about parent-teen relationships from the parent's side? from the teen's side?
- What is enjoyable about parent-teen relationships from the parent's side? from the teen's side?

Close the discussion with a few minutes of quiet reflection on relationships with parents.

3. Letters from parents: If you have not received a letter for a retreatant, have a staff member write an affirming letter for her or him. This retreatant might need extra support because she or he will probably feel left out, angry at the parent(s), or sad about the particular circumstances that led to no letter being written by a parent.

Introduce this activity by saying something like the following: "Your parents have written letters to express their love and concern for you. Some parents might not express their love in a manner expected by you. If after reading the letter you find this is the case, try to trust your parent's sincerity and read between the lines."

Pass out the letters. Encourage the retreatants to find a quiet place to read their letter alone. Give the retreatants about fifteen minutes to read their letter.

Be alert for retreatants who may be upset because their letter was not affirming and raised some sensitive issues. They might need some support.

Build the campfire while the retreatants are reading the letters.

4. *Campfire:* Gather the retreatants in a circle around the campfire. Invite the retreatants to talk about their feelings. Respect the privacy of the letters and stay with feelings. Notice if any attitudes have changed as a result of the letters.

5. *Closure:* Offer a prayer of thanks for families, especially parents.

10:00 p.m. Campfire

Relax around the campfire. Hot chocolate and s'mores are a nice addition. End the evening with a brief prayer. See handout 10-C, "Evening Prayer for Day 2," for a suggested prayer. If the lighting permits reading, distribute the handout to the group.

11:00 p.m. Closedown

One staff person announces the schedule for day 3 and makes any other announcements.

Retreat Activities: Day 3

7:30 a.m. Wake-up

8:00 a.m. Breakfast

Team 2 prepares the meal. One staff person should be available to make announcements and to choose a retreatant to lead the group in prayer.

Team 1 cleans up after breakfast, while team 3 prepares the lunch that will be taken on the hike.

9:00 a.m. Morning prayer

During day 2 of the retreat, the retreatants focused on the works of God in nature. During day 3, they will concentrate on the gift of friends in their life. The morning prayer again sets the tone for the day.

Staff: one person

Materials needed: Bibles, journals, pens, and the song "Spirit of God," by Maranatha Music

Description of activities

1. Explain to the retreatants that the purpose of this activity is to give them an opportunity to reflect upon God's love as shared with them through the gift of friends.

2. If a musician is available to accompany the group, lead the retreatants in singing "Spirit of God," by Maranatha Music. This song is short and simple, so the retreatants do not need songbooks.

If no musician is available, offer a short opening prayer: "Spirit of God, we feel your presence as we sit surrounded by our friends and the beauty of the natural surroundings. Thank you for the love we know through our family and friends. Be with us this day as we continue to open our mind and heart to the many gifts you have showered upon us. We pray this morning in the name of Jesus, our Lord. Amen."

3. Invite the retreatants to review their past and present friendships. Ask the retreatants to recall each year from the time they were five years old until the present and to list in their journal the name and the specific memories of each person that comes to mind. After they list these, instruct the retreatants to silently think about each person listed and to offer a prayer for them. Allow plenty of quiet time for this activity.

4. Encourage the retreatants to thank God throughout the day as more friendship memories come to mind.

5. Invite the retreatants to read silently Ps. 34: 1–11.

9:30 a.m. Pack for hike

See the list of supplies given for hike 1 on page 93.

10:00 a.m. Hike 2

Plan to take the retreatants on a new trail for hike 2. A new trail offers new opportunities for exploring the beauty of the natural surroundings. Before beginning the hike, tell the retreatants to be on the lookout for a symbol of the holy ground on which they have been living. Explain that these symbols will be for the Offertory of the closing liturgy tomorrow. This symbol can be a rock, a stone, a branch, a piece of bark—as long as its removal does not disturb the natural environment. Suggest that it be something that can be taken home as a memento of the retreat.

12:30 p.m. Lunch and recreation

One staff person should be available to make announcements and to choose a retreatant to lead the group in prayer before the meal. Be sure to carry back all trash.

2:00 p.m. Hike 2 (return to camp)

5:00 p.m. Dinner preparation

Team 4 prepares the meal. Other retreatants can use this time to explore or relax. Some retreatants might gather firewood. Remind the retreatants of the safety guidelines mentioned earlier.

6:00 p.m. Dinner

One staff person should be available to make announcements and to choose a retreatant to lead the group in prayer before the meal.

Team 5 cleans up after the meal.

7:30 p.m. Evening prayer

The evening prayer is an opportunity for the group to offer prayers of thanks for the gifts of the day. There is no break between the prayer and the affirmation activity that follows. Affirmation will be an emotional and long activity, so the evening prayer should be simple and low-key.

Staff: one person to lead the prayer. All staff members should participate.

Materials needed: none

Description of activities: Gather the retreatants into a circle. Invite them to quietly reflect on the gifts of the day. After a few minutes of silence, invite everyone to offer a spontaneous prayer of thanks. After the prayers, move directly into the next activity.

7:45 p.m. Affirmation

A campfire can be built at the beginning of this activity.

Staff: one person to lead the activity. All staff members should participate.

Materials needed: none

Description of activities

1. Explain to the retreatants the value of noticing the gifts of God as they are received in the here and now by saying something like the following: "We often reflect on the gifts God has showered on us in the past, but it is important to notice the gifts we are enjoying in the present. Then, especially when the gifts are in the form of persons, we can affirm them and be grateful for them directly, rather than only appreciating them after they are gone."

2. Ask the retreatants to recognize and seriously think about the gifts received through each person on the retreat. Suggest they write these in their journal so they have specifics in mind when it is time to affirm others.

3. Focus on one retreatant at a time. Ask each retreatant to speak directly in affirmation to that person. After everyone has addressed this person, ask if she or he would like to make a statement to the group. Do this affirmation for each retreatant. (In this type of process, each retreatant is affirmed to the degree that she or he is known by the others. Because this activity comes near the end of the retreat, most retreatants are known pretty well by the others.)

4. Encourage the retreatants to make affirmation a part of all their relationships and to thank God regularly for gifts received.

10:30 p.m. Campfire

This is a time to relax. Hot chocolate can be served. Gather the retreatants around the campfire. If a musician (a retreatant or a staff member who has brought an instrument) is available, she or he can lead retreatants in singing familiar songs. Songbooks or handouts are not necessary for this activity. If no one wants to sing or tell camp stories, then encourage the retreatants to sit around the campfire talking to one another. End the evening with a spontaneous prayer of thanks.

11:00 p.m. Closedown

One staff person announces the schedule for day 4 and makes any other announcements.

Retreat Activities: Day 4

7:30 a.m. Wake-up

8:00 a.m. Breakfast

Team 7 prepares the meal. One staff person should be available to make announcements and to choose a retreatant to lead the group in prayer before the meal. Team 6 cleans up after the meal.

9:00 a.m. Cleanup

Take down tents, load the bus or the cars, and arrange the campsite tables as they were upon arrival.

10:00 a.m. Liturgy

The purpose of having the liturgy at the end of the retreat is to celebrate and bless again the holy ground that was home for four days. As the retreatants worship together, the bonds they have formed deepen.

During the Prayer of the Faithful, invite the retreatants to offer a prayer of thanks for something special that happened during the retreat.

At offertory time, have the retreatants present their symbol of the ground on which they have been living, such as a rock, a stone, a branch, or a piece of bark. Suggest that they take their symbol home as a memento of the retreat.

Consider using the following opening song and readings:
- opening song: "Holy Ground" from the album *Be Exalted*, by John Michael Talbot, or "Holy Ground" from the album *Read the Book, Don't Wait for the Movie*, by Whiteheart
- first reading: 2 Cor. 13:11–13
- response: "Lord, send out your Spirit and renew the face of the earth," with Ps. 104:1,24,29–30, 31,34
- gospel reading: John 20:19–23

11:00 a.m. Departure

The departure is at an early hour because it is assumed the travel time is significant. Upon arriving home, gather to pray in thanksgiving for a safe journey. The following prayer is suggested:

> Lord, we are home again,
>   and we lift up our hearts in a song of gratitude
>   for the blessings of our journey.
> . . . .
>
> You have been our personal escort upon this journey.
> We are grateful
>   for all we have seen and experienced,
>   for the beauty we have met,
>   for the new places we have visited.
>
> We are thankful, also,
>   for the protection from harm and injury that was ours.
> . . . .
>
> Lord, it is good to be home again.
> Our time away has opened our eyes
>   to see our home and belongings
>   with greater appreciation.
> Since half of the pleasure of a journey
>   is in the coming home,
>   we take joy in our return.
>
> May this joy
>   be a taste of the happiness awaiting us
>   when we finally come home to You.
> . . . .
>
> We pause now
>   and, in silence, lift up our hearts in gratitude
>   for the pleasures of our trip
>   and the blessing of being home.
>
> [Pause for silent prayer.]
>
> Blessed are You, Lord of All Who Travel,
>   for Your holy and gracious care while we traveled
>   and for bringing us home safely again.
> Amen.

(Hays, *Prayers for the Domestic Church*, p. 37)

Sample 10-A

Letter to Parents

Dear [**name of parent or guardian**]:

As you know, your son or daughter [**name**] will be participating in the upcoming camping retreat. During the evening of the second day of retreat, the retreatants will be reflecting upon relationships with their parents. After the discussion, we would like to give to the retreatants a letter of affirmation from you. Would you help us to prepare for this activity?

Please write a letter to your son or daughter expressing your positive feelings toward him or her. You might recall happy episodes of his or her childhood and include these in the letter. This is meant to be a letter of affirmation, so it would not be appropriate to discuss problem areas of your relationship in this letter. This can be done some other time.

Please send the letter to me by [**date**], at the following address: [**address**].

Because these letters are to be a surprise for the retreatants, please do not leave this letter where your son or daughter might see it.

Thank you for your support. Please pray for the retreatants, especially when they receive your letter at 7:30 p.m. on the second day of the retreat.

Sincerely,

[Your name]

Blessed Are You, Lord Our God, for Silence and Solitude

Blessed are You, Lord our God,
    who gives to us nourishment
        in times of silence and solitude.

From uplifted hearts, hearts full of gratitude,
    may this prayer of thanksgiving rise to You,
    God of All Gifts and of Great Generosity.

We are thankful for times of stillness
    which allow us to listen
    to that holy river of prayer
    flowing in the heart;
    for the presence
    of Your Holy Spirit within,
    the Spirit who prays continuously.

These times of quiet heal us, within and without,
    replenish our spirit with new strength
    and prepare us to meet the constant struggle of daily life
    with renewed hope and joy.

Like Your Son, Jesus,
    who climbed mountains at night,
    who retreated deep into the desert
    to find You in stillness,
    may we,
    after this silent-solitary communion with You,
    allow our lives to reveal
    Your glory and grace.

Lord, may the seeds of the tree of stillness
    bear fruit for us
    and for all the restless world.

Blessed are You, Lord our God,
    who gives to us nourishment
    in times of silence and solitude.

Amen.

(Hays, *Prayers for the Domestic Church,* p. 58)

Handout 10–A: Permission to reproduce this handout is granted.

Meal Duties

Team 1
Day 1: Dinner preparation
Day 3: Breakfast cleanup
Menu:
Adult supervisor: _____

Retreatants: 1. _____
               2. _____
               3. _____
               4. _____

Team 2
Day 1: Dinner cleanup
Day 3: Breakfast preparation
Menu:
Adult supervisor: _____

Retreatants: 1. _____
               2. _____
               3. _____
               4. _____

Team 3
Day 2: Breakfast preparation
Day 3: Lunch preparation
Breakfast menu:
Lunch menu:
Adult supervisor: _____

Retreatants: 1. _____
               2. _____
               3. _____
               4. _____

Team 4
Day 2: Breakfast cleanup
Day 3: Dinner preparation
Menu:
Adult supervisor: _____

Retreatants: 1. _____
               2. _____
               3. _____
               4. _____

Team 5
Day 2: Lunch preparation
Day 3: Dinner cleanup
Menu:
Adult supervisor: _____

Retreatants: 1. _____
               2. _____
               3. _____
               4. _____

Team 6
Day 2: Dinner preparation
Day 4: Breakfast cleanup
Menu:
Adult supervisor: _____

Retreatants: 1. _____
               2. _____
               3. _____
               4. _____

Team 7
Day 2: Dinner cleanup
Day 4: Breakfast preparation
Menu:
Adult supervisor: _____

Retreatants: 1. _____
               2. _____
               3. _____
               4. _____

Evening Prayer

My Lord, Beloved Source of All That Is,
    I bow before You as I come to the end of my day.
The sun has journeyed across the sky
    and has disappeared beneath the horizon.
This day is now complete,
    and I greet the darkness of night
        with a prayer of gratitude.
I thank You for all the sun-touched gifts of this day.

[*Pause for silent reflection.*]

I ask Your mercy for the times, this day,
    when I have forgotten to be kind and compassionate.
I am sorry for the times
    when I have rushed through the mystery of life,
        blind to the needs of others
        or to the beauties of creation.

[*Pause for silent reflection.*]

In a communion with stars, planets and moons,
    in communion with all the servants of God,
        may I enter into sacred stillness.

[*Pause for silent reflection.*]

My Lord and God,
    Cosmic Creator of both the Sun and Moon,
    I praise and adore You.
In divine wisdom, You have balanced all of creation,
    day and night, male and female,
    summer and winter, light and dark.
I embrace that balance
    and, in this day that is closing,
        have attempted to balance the needs of body and spirit,
        the demands of the inner person and the public person.
Wrapped in gratitude,
    I now place before You my personal needs: _____
_____
    (as well as the needs of others: _____
_____).

Lord of Day and Night, of Life and Death,
    I place myself into Your holy hands.

(Hays, *Prayers for the Domestic Church,* p. 163)

Part F ▽

Retreat Follow-ups

Retreat follow-up programs provide the retreatants with an opportunity to gather again as a Christian community. During these gatherings, the retreatants recall the retreat experience, renew friendships, and discuss their progress on their retreat resolutions. A retreat follow-up program should take place within four weeks after a retreat.

Follow-up programs may be important for some retreats, but not others. You will need to determine when a follow-up is appropriate and which type of program is most suitable.

There are three retreat follow-up programs presented in this part of the manual.

"An Afternoon Gathering" is a program designed for an after-school meeting of retreatants. It provides the time for the retreatants to recall the retreat and to pray together.

"An Evening with Parents" is a program designed to help the retreatants recall the retreat experience and share this experience with their parents. This program also gives the parents a chance to talk with other parents.

"An Evening Potluck" is a program designed to help the retreatants recall the retreat experience and deepen their relationships with one another by sharing a meal, a liturgy, and an informal social.

11

An Afternoon Gathering

"An Afternoon Gathering" is a two-hour program designed for an after-school meeting of the retreatants. High school students can have difficulty finding a time to meet for a retreat follow-up. Right after school might be the best time for many of them.

The goals of this retreat follow-up are the following:
- That the retreatants reflect on the retreat experience
- That the retreatants discuss their retreat resolutions
- That the retreatants pray together as a Christian community

Schedule

3:30 p.m.   Arrival
3:45 p.m.   Introduction and prayer
4:00 p.m.   Dyad discussion: Postretreat experiences
4:30 p.m.   Large-group discussion: Feedback
5:15 p.m.   Closing prayer
5:30 p.m.   Departure

Materials needed: the retreat schedule, a tape player and a tape, song sheets, and copies of handouts

Follow-up Program Activities

3:30 p.m. Arrival

Two staff members are available to welcome the retreatants. Other staff members who worked at the retreat can mingle with the group.

3:45 p.m. Introduction and prayer

Because this retreat follow-up program is short, the introduction, which includes a review of the retreat schedule, is important. It sets the tone for the afternoon. Reviewing the retreat activities helps the retreatants recall their experience of the retreat. This recalling, in turn, helps the discussions that come later in the schedule.

You might liven up this activity by mentioning some memorable incidents or insights from the retreat. Also, invite the retreatants to share incidents that are memorable for them.

Staff: two people (including one person to assist with the distribution of handouts)

Materials needed: copies of a prayer handout used during the retreat or handout 11–A, a copy of the retreat schedule, a tape player, and a music tape used during the retreat

Description of activities

1. Opening prayer: You might use a prayer handout from the retreat. It will help the retreatants recall the theme and the retreat experience. If one is not available, use handout 11–A, "Opening Prayer: Psalm 67."

2. *Follow-up schedule:* Introduce the program by saying something such as this: "This afternoon we have gathered to recall our retreat experience and to pray together again as a Christian community. The schedule for this afternoon's program is only two hours long, and it is very full.

"I would like to begin by reviewing the activities of your retreat experience a month ago. As I review the schedule of activities, try to recall the thoughts and feelings that you had during the retreat. After the review, you will have some time to talk about your recollections."

3. *Review:* Review the retreat schedule. Pause after naming each activity. If appropriate, you might play in the background a tape of music that was used during the retreat.

4. *Closure:* End with a few minutes of quiet. Then introduce the next activity.

4:00 p.m. Dyad discussion: Postretreat experiences

This dyad activity is designed to help the retreatants recall their retreat experience and discuss their postretreat experience. The pairing technique helps to give each person the time to speak and to support another person.

Staff: two people (including one person to assist with the distribution of handouts)

Materials needed: handout 11-B

Description of activities

1. *Introduction:* Explain that the purpose of the activity is to provide the retreatants with an opportunity to talk with one another about retreat and postretreat experiences.

2. *Dyads:* Pair the retreatants randomly. Have them decide who will speak first (this person is referred to as *partner A* below). Explain the process in the following way: Each partner will be given a set of discussion questions and an opportunity to look them over. Then partner A speaks to partner B by responding to the questions; B simply listens for ten minutes. Next B speaks to A; A simply listens for ten minutes. Finally, A and B speak to each other with no structure.

Distribute handout 11-B, "Dyad Discussion Questions." Tell the retreatants when to begin their speaking and announce the time changes during the discussion.

3. *Closure:* Gather the retreatants into a large group and begin the next activity.

4:30 p.m. Large-group discussion: Feedback

This large-group discussion helps the retreatants put closure on the afternoon experience by sharing thoughts and hearing from others. Because the group is large and time is limited, encourage brief comments.

Staff: one person

Materials needed: none

Description of activities

1. *Guidelines:* Review the discussion guidelines developed during the retreat. Include confidentiality, respect, no putdowns, honesty, trust, and an attempt to participate by all.

2. *Discussion:* Facilitate the discussion by using the questions suggested below. Ask one question at a time. Invite a response from everyone. Point out similarities and differences in the answers.
- What thoughts and feelings came to you while you were talking with your dyad partner?
- Has the retreat made any difference in your life? Explain.
- What can you do to support other retreatants?
- How can the retreat community support you?

3. *Summary:* Summarize the discussion.

5:15 p.m. Closing prayer

The closing prayer is designed to reinforce community among the retreatants. Choose a song-prayer that contains the theme of the retreat. If such a song-prayer was part of the retreat, use it.

Staff: one person

Materials needed: song sheets, and a tape player and a tape

Description of activities

Invite the retreatants to join in song as a way of praying. Thank the retreatants for participating in the retreat follow-up and encourage them to continue to pray for one another.

5:30 p.m. Departure

Opening Prayer: Psalm 67

May we continually be
    the recipients of God's mercy and blessing
in order that we may demonstrate
    God's order and purpose throughout the earth
    and God's redemptive power
       to the creatures of this world.

And may it ultimately resolve
   in all of God's children lifting their voices
     in praise to their Lord and God.

The nations of the earth would truly
    abide in peace and sing for joy
  if they would direct their destinies
    according to God's will.
Then the inhabitants of this world would surely
  lift their voices in praise to their Lord and God.

The earth continues to receive
  the abundance of God.
God's blessings are all about us.

May every mountain and valley, plain and forest,
  every city with its teeming apartments,
  and every sprawling suburb
    echo with the praises of all to their God.

    (Adapted from Brandt, *Psalms/Now,* p. 107)

Dyad Discussion Questions

Directions: Read over the following questions. At the signal from your leader, one of the partners responds to the questions. The other partner simply listens. After ten minutes, your leader will signal you to change roles—the person who was speaking now listens and the person who was listening now speaks. After another ten minutes, your leader will signal you to begin to talk with your partner freely. Your discussion can continue until your leader calls all of the retreatants together in one large group.

1. How do you feel about being here today?
2. What were your thoughts during the review of the retreat schedule?
3. What feelings surfaced during the review of the retreat schedule?
4. Regarding your retreat resolution, how have things been going since the retreat?
5. What have been positive postretreat experiences for you?
6. What have been difficult postretreat experiences for you?

12

An Evening with Parents

"An Evening with Parents" is a three-hour program for retreatants and their parents. It is designed to encourage young retreatants to share significant retreat experiences with their parents.

The goals of this retreat follow-up are the following:
- That the retreatants recall and discuss their retreat resolutions
- That the parents discuss with other parents the changes they have seen in their son or daughter since the retreat
- That the retreatants and parents pray together as a Christian community

Schedule

7:00 p.m.   Arrival
7:30 p.m.   Introduction and prayer
8:00 p.m.   Small-group discussion: Postretreat experiences
8:45 p.m.   Break
9:00 p.m.   Large-group discussion: Feedback
9:30 p.m.   Social
10:00 p.m. Departure

Materials needed: Hot and cold drinks, desserts, a slide projector, a screen, slides taken during the retreat, a tape recorder, a tape of a song used during the retreat, a Bible, blank name tags, pens, and copies of a prayer handout used during the retreat

Follow-up Program Activities

7:00 p.m. Arrival

Two staff members are available to welcome the retreatants and their parents and to have them fill out name tags. Other staff members who worked at the retreat can mingle with the group.

Hot and cold beverages are available at this time.

7:30 p.m. Introduction and prayer

The introduction is a time to welcome the retreatants and their parents. Showing slides and playing music from the retreat will help the retreatants recall the retreat experience, and it also can be an effective way to share the retreat experience with the parents.

Staff: two people (including one to assist with the distribution of handouts)

Materials needed: slides, a slide projector, a screen, a tape player, an appropriate tape, copies of a prayer handout used during the retreat

Description of activities

1. Prayer: Lead the community in prayer. Hand out copies of a prayer that was used during the retreat.

2. Explanation of the activity: Introduce the program by saying something like the following: "Retreatants, we gather this evening to recall a very special experience in our life—the retreat we experienced together one month ago. You shared a tremendous amount with one another at the retreat. You prayed together. You played together.

You discussed personal experiences and concerns. You formed new friendships. Tonight's activities will help deepen the meanings of the retreat and reinforce the bonds you made.

"Parents, during the past month, you too have participated in your son's or daughter's retreat by experiencing the effects the retreat has had in your son's or daughter's life. Tonight's activities will help you to continue to share more fully your son's or daughter's life.

"We all struggle at times to find the words to express our love for one another. Coming together here tonight does already say a lot about the care that we have for one another. Later on we might wish to express more explicitly the feelings that we have for one another.

"Tonight's schedule consists of a slide presentation, a discussion, and time to socialize. Please feel free to participate in the activities only to the degree that you are comfortable."

3. Slides: Explain the retreat theme and run the slide presentation. Play a song, preferably one used at the retreat, for background music.

4. Introductions: Introduce the staff.

8:00 p.m. Small-group discussion: Postretreat experiences

This discussion is designed to build support among the retreatants. Assign small groups for this discussion activity. Divide the parents into groups of eight. Separate related couples. Assign the retreatants to the same small groups as during the retreat. If all of the retreatants are not present and the groups have less than seven members, form new groups.

Staff: one person for each small group

Materials needed: none

Description of activities

1. Introductions: In the parent groups, invite each person to introduce herself or himself to the group.

2. Guidelines: Review small-group discussion guidelines that were made during the retreat. Include confidentiality, respect, no putdowns, honesty, trust, and an attempt to participate by all. Inform the parents that these guidelines were developed by the retreatants during the retreat.

3. Discussion: Facilitate group discussion by using the questions suggested below. Ask one question at a time. Point out similarities and differences in the responses. Encourage the group members to ask one another questions about their postretreat experience.

Discussion questions for parents:
- What kinds of changes did you expect to see in your son or daughter as a result of the retreat?
- What changes have you noticed in your son or daughter since the retreat?
- What changes have you noticed in yourself since your son or daughter returned from the retreat?
- How do you want to continue to support your son or daughter in his or her retreat resolutions?

Discussion questions for retreatants:
- What memories and feelings surfaced while you viewed the slides?
- What changes have you noticed in yourself since the retreat?
- What changes have you noticed in your parents since the retreat?
- What have been good experiences for you since the retreat?
- What have been difficult experiences for you since the retreat?
- What do you need in the way of support to keep alive your retreat resolutions?

4. Summary: Summarize the discussion. Invite each group member to make a closing comment.

5. Closure: Invite a group member to lead the closing prayer.

8:45 p.m. Break

9:00 p.m. Large-group discussion: Feedback

This discussion gives both the parents and the retreatants an opportunity to speak to the whole group about their feelings and thoughts from the small-group discussions. It also gives both groups an opportunity to hear what the others discussed.

Staff: one person

Materials needed: none

Description of activities

1. Introduction: Explain that the purpose of this activity is to give the parents and the retreatants a chance to express their thoughts and feelings about retreat and postretreat experiences.

2. Discussion: Invite the parents and the retreatants to express their responses to the questions asked in the small-group discussion. If the group is large, you might begin by having one person from each small group summarize the discussion of his or her small group. Then you can open the exchange to the whole group for the remaining time.

3. Closure: Lead the group in praying together the Lord's Prayer and exchanging the sign of peace.

9:30 p.m. Social

This informal gathering gives the retreatants time to introduce friends to their parents and vice versa. It also allows parents and retreatants to continue any discussions that began during the small groups. Have desserts and drinks available.

10:00 p.m. Departure

13

An Evening Potluck

"An Evening Potluck" is a five-and-one-half-hour program best used on evenings when retreatants are most free of other events.

The goals of this retreat follow-up are the following:
- That the retreatants celebrate a eucharistic liturgy
- That the retreatants discuss their retreat resolutions
- That the retreatants renew friendships, especially during the socializing session

Schedule

5:00 p.m.   Arrival
5:30 p.m.   Introduction
5:45 p.m.   Liturgy
6:30 p.m.   Break
6:45 p.m.   Dinner
7:45 p.m.   Small-group discussion: Relationships and retreat resolutions
8:45 p.m.   Roundup
9:00 p.m.   Social
10:30 p.m. Departure

Materials needed:

Food: Request the retreatants to bring food for the potluck (suggest that people with names beginning with A–H bring main dishes; I–P, salads; and Q–Z, desserts). Provide beverages and snacks for the social

For the liturgy: a chalice, a plate, bread, wine, water, a corporal, a purificator, a candle, matches, a Bible, the sacramentary, music books, and copies of the program (*Note:* Arrange for the services of a priest.)

Miscellaneous: blank name tags, copies of handouts, trash bags, plates, cups, napkins, forks and knives, a tape player, and tapes with music for the social

Follow-up Program Activities

5:00 p.m. Arrival

Two staff members are available to welcome the retreatants, to have them fill out name tags, and to direct them as to where to put the food for the potluck dinner. Other staff members who worked on the retreat can mingle with the group.

Choose retreatants to help with the various parts of the liturgy. The parts of the liturgy include the following:
- reading the first reading
- reading the response
- presenting the offertory gifts
- serving as eucharistic minister

5:30 p.m. Introduction

This introduction is designed to be short because it is followed immediately by the liturgy.

Staff: one person

Materials needed: none

Description of activities

Say something like the following to introduce the program: "One month ago, we left our busy schedules to make a retreat to renew our relationships with God and with other persons. This evening we gather to support one another in continuing this effort. The retreat may seem to have been so long ago that it is hard to recall the feelings and the meanings of those days. Tonight, together, we will recall the retreat experience and take a look at the resolutions we made there. You will be able to discuss with each other how you might continue in working toward those retreat resolutions."

Remind the retreatants about the theme of the retreat.

5:45 p.m. Liturgy

Choose readings and songs that were used during the retreat. This helps the retreatants to recall the retreat experience. Individuals carry out those parts of the Mass for which they are responsible.

6:30 p.m. Break

Two staff members are available to supervise putting out the food.

6:45 p.m. Dinner

One staff person should be available to choose a retreatant to lead the prayer before the meal.

7:45 p.m. Small-group discussion: Relationships and retreat resolutions

During this activity, the leader facilitates the retreatants in a reexamination of their relationship with God and a renewal of their retreat resolution.

Assign the retreatants to small groups. Consider forming small groups different from the groups formed during the retreat.

Staff: one person to lead each small group

Materials needed: none

Description of activities

1. Introductions: Invite each retreatant to introduce, or reintroduce, himself or herself to the group.

2. Guidelines: Review the small-group discussion guidelines that were developed during the retreat. Include confidentiality, no putdowns, honesty, trust, and an attempt to participate by all.

3. Discussion: Facilitate a discussion using the questions suggested below. You might ask each member of the group the first two questions and then address the rest of the questions to the group as a whole.
- How have your relationships (with God, self, family, friends) been since the retreat?
- What do you want to do to strengthen any of these relationships?
- What was your retreat resolution?
- Do you wish to renew this resolution or make a new one in light of what this past month has shown you?

4. Summary: Summarize the discussion and invite each group member to make a closing comment.

5. Closure: Invite a group member to offer a closing prayer.

8:45 p.m. Roundup

This activity helps the retreatants to put some closure on the serious discussions held in their small groups and enables them to move freely to the social.

Staff: one person

Materials needed: none

Description of activities

Explain that the purpose of the activity is to give the retreatants an opportunity to make closing comments to the large group. Arrange the group in a circle and, moving around the circle, invite the retreatants to express their thoughts and feelings about their retreat follow-up experience.

Announce the next activity.

9:00 p.m. Social

Play music and serve snacks and beverages.

10:30 p.m. Departure

Resources ▽

Books

Chapter 4

Bemmel, John Van. *Lenten Conversations with God.* Mystic, CT: Twenty-Third Publications, 1985.

Powers, Isaias. *A Personal Way of the Cross.* Mystic, CT: Twenty-Third Publications, 1987.

———. *Scripture Meditations for Lent.* Mystic, CT: Twenty-Third Publications, 1987. Updated annually.

Chapter 5

Dear, John. *Disarming the Heart.* New York: Paulist Press, 1987. Documents of Vatican Council II.

Saint Vincent Pallotti Center for Apostolic Development. *Connections.* Washington, DC: Saint Vincent Pallotti Center for Apostolic Development. An annual directory of lay volunteer service opportunities. The center's address is 715 Monroe Street, NE, Washington, DC 20017-1755. Phone: 202-529-3330.

Teresa, Mother. *Words to Love By . . . .* Notre Dame, IN: Ave Maria Press, 1983.

Chapter 6

Bridges, William. *Transitions.* Reading, MA: Addison-Wesley Publishing, 1980.

Peck, M. Scott. *The Road Less Traveled.* New York: Simon and Schuster, 1978.

Chapter 7

Angelica, Mother M. *The Promised Woman.* Birmingham, AL: Journey into Scripture, 1977.

Donders, Joseph G. *A Star Rising: Advent Meditations.* Mystic, CT: Twenty-Third Publications. 1986.

John Paul II. "Redemptoris Mater," 25 March 1987.

Johnson, Ann. *Miryam of Nazareth: Woman of Strength and Wisdom.* Notre Dame, IN: Ave Maria Press, 1984.

Montfort, St. Louis de. *True Devotion to Mary.* Rockford, IL: Tan Books, 1985.

Polek, David, and Rita Anderhub. *Advent Begins at Home: Family Prayers and Activities.* Liguori, MO: Liguori Publications, 1979.

Powers, Isaias. *Daily Scripture Meditations for Advent.* Mystic, CT: Twenty-Third Publications, 1985. Updated annually.

Chapter 8

Al-Anon Family Group Headquarters. *Al-Anon's Twelve Steps and Twelve Traditions.* New York: Al-Anon Family Group Headquarters, 1986.

Alcoholics Anonymous World Services. *Alcoholics Anonymous.* New York: Alcoholics Anonymous World Services, 1986.

Gibbs, Jeanne, and Andre Allen. *Tribes: A Process for Peer Involvement.* Oakland, CA: Center Source Publications, 1978.

Hazelden Educational Materials. Catalogs of books, pamphlets, films, and audiocassettes can be obtained by writing to Hazelden at Box 176, Center City, MN 55102. Phone: 800-328-9000.

National Clearinghouse for Alcohol Information, Box 2345, Rockville, MD 20850.

National Clearinghouse for Drug Abuse Information, Box 1635, Rockville, MD 20850.

Rosellini, Gayle, and Mark Worden. *Of Course You're Angry: A Family Guide to Dealing with the Emotions of Chemical Dependence.* San Francisco: Harper and Row, 1985.

Tessler, Diane Jane. *Drugs, Kids and Schools: Practical Strategies for Educators and Other Concerned Adults.* Glenview, IL: Scott, Foresman and Co., 1980.

W., Claire. *God, Help Me Stop.* San Diego, CA: Books West, 1982. A twelve-step Bible-study workbook for any addiction.

Woititz, Janet Geringer. *Adult Children of Alcoholics.* Pompano Beach, FL: Health Communications, 1983.

Chapter 9

Culligan, Kevin G., ed. *Spiritual Direction: Contemporary Readings.* Locust Valley, NY: Living Flame Press, 1983.

Doherty, Catherine de Hueck. *Poustinia: Christian Spirituality of the East for Western Man.* Notre Dame, IN: Ave Maria Press, 1975.

Doyle, Brendan. *Meditations with Julian of Norwich.* Sante Fe, NM: Bear and Co., 1983.

Edwards, Tilden. *Spiritual Friend: Reclaiming the Gift of Spiritual Direction.* New York: Paulist Press, 1980.

Hutchinson, Gloria. *Christ Encounters.* Notre Dame, IN: Ave Maria Press, 1985.

Mazziotta, Richard. *Jesus in the Gospels: Old Stories Told Anew.* Notre Dame, IN: Ave Maria Press, 1986.

Mello, Anthony de. *Wellsprings.* Garden City, NY: Doubleday and Co., 1985.

Ward, Benedicta. *The Desert Christian: The Sayings of the Desert Fathers.* New York: Macmillan Publishing, 1975.

Chapter 10

Hart, John. *Walking Softly in the Wilderness—The Sierra Club Guide to Backpacking.* San Francisco: Sierra Club Books, 1977.

Hays, Edward. *Prayers for the Domestic Church.* Easton, KS: Forest of Peace Books, 1979.

Marriott, Alice, and Carol K. Rachlin. *American Indian Mythology.* New York: New American Library, 1968.

Sandi, Michael. *Sports Illustrated Backpacking.* New York: Harper and Row, 1980.

Park Information

National Park Service
U.S. Department of the Interior
Washington, DC 20240

Other sources of information on parks are state and regional parks and commercial outfitters. For topographic maps of the United States east of the Mississippi River, contact Branch of Distribution, U.S. Geological Survey, 1200 South Eads Street, Arlington, VA 22202. For maps of the United States west of the Mississippi River, contact Branch of Distribution, U.S. Geological Survey, Box 25286, Federal Center, Denver, CO 80225.

General

Adams, James E., ed. *Living Words: Daily Meditations for Catholics.* Saint Louis, MO: Creative Communications for the Parish. Published quarterly.

Adamson, Dave, and Steve Hunt. *Youth Ministry Clip Art.* Loveland, CO: Group Books, 1987.

Anderson, Yohann, comp. *Songs.* San Anselmo, CA: Songs and Creations, 1978.

Berkus, Rusty. *To Heal Again.* Encino, CA: Red Rose Press, 1984. On healing and forgiveness.

Doyle, Aileen A. *Youth Retreats: Creating Sacred Space for Young People.* Winona, MN: Saint Mary's Press, 1986.

Ensley, Eddie. *Prayer That Heals Our Emotions.* Columbus, GA: Contemplative Books, 1986.

Fluegelman, Andrew, ed. *More New Games and Playful Ideas.* Garden City, NY: Doubleday and Co., 1981. For designing icebreakers.

———. *The New Games Book.* Garden City, NY: Doubleday and Co., 1976. For designing icebreakers.

Gilmour, Peter. *Praying Together.* Winona, MN: Saint Mary's Press, 1978.

Harrah, Walt, Chuck Fromm, and Stan Endicott, comp. *Maranatha!* Dallas: Word, Inc., 1987.

McKillop, Tom. *What's Happening to My Life?* New York: Paulist Press, 1986.

Maranatha! Music. *Marantha! Music Praise and Worship Collection.* Costa Mesa, CA: Maranatha! Music, 1987.

Mello, Anthony de. *The Song of the Bird.* Garden City, NY: Image Books, 1984.

North American Liturgy Resources. *Glory and Praise*. Phoenix, AZ: North American Liturgy Resources, 1980.

Parmisano, Stan. *Come to the Mountain: The Contemporary Experience of Prayer*. Notre Dame, IN: Ave Maria Press, 1986.

Reichter, Arlo. *The Group Retreat Book*. Loveland, CO: Group Books, 1983.

Rice, Wayne, and Mike Yaconelli. *Incredible Ideas for Youth Groups*. Grand Rapids, MI: Zondervan Publishing House, 1982.

Thom Schultz Publications. *Group Magazine*. Box 481, Loveland, CO 80539. Phone: 303-669-3836.

Weinstein, Matt. *Playfair: Everybody's Guide to Noncompetitive Play*. San Luis Obispo, CA: Impact Publishers, 1980.

Audiovisual Materials

Meditation Program. Saint John's Abbey, Collegeville, MN: Liturgical Press. A series of three meditations, each containing slides, a cassette, and a script.
- Meditation 1: saints, thanksgiving, death
- Meditation 2: state, penance, family
- Meditation 3: earth, spirit, prayer

Slide Meditations. Vol. 1. Center for Learning, P.O. Box 910, Villa Maria, PA 16155. Themes include prayer and solitude, God's good earth, nature's beauty, nature's life cycle, faith, our universe, friendship and love, new beginnings, adolescent relationships, despair and death, people at play, social needs, joy, the Holy Land, and lights in the night.

Music

Instrumentals

Barry, John. *Out of Africa* and *Somewhere in Time* (movie soundtracks).

The Dameans, *Reflections*.

Keaggy, Phil. *Wind and the Wheat*.

Lanz, David, and Michael Jones. *Winter Solstice* (piano solos with a Christmas theme).

Mehler and Nash, *Jazz Praise*.

Vangelis. *Chariots of Fire* (movie soundtrack).

Winston, George. *Winter into Spring*.

Contemporary Christian Artists and Albums

Andrus and Blackwood. *Holiday*.

Boone, Debby. *Choose Life*.

Card, Michael. *Legacy*, *Known By the Scars*, and *First Light*.

DeSario, Teri. *A Call to Us*.

Duncan, Bryan. *Whislin' in the Dark*.

Franzak, Tom. *Shadowboxing* and *Walk That Talk*.

The Bill Gaither Trio. *Welcome Back Home* and *Ten New Songs with the Bill Gaither Trio*.

Grant, Amy. *Lead Me On*, *The Collection*, *Straight Ahead*, *Unguarded*, *Amy Grant in Concert*, *My Father's Eyes*, *Age to Age*, and *Amy Grant in Concert*, vol. 2.

Keaggy, Phil. *Play thru Me*, *Town to Town*, and *Ph'Lip Side Kids for Kids About Life*.

Maranatha Music. *Praise 1*, *Praise 2*, *Praise 3*, *Praise 4*, *Praise 5*, *Praise 6*, *Praise 7*, *Praise 8*, and *Praise 9*.

Patillo, Leon. *The Sky's the Limit*.

Patti, Sandi. *More Than Wonderful*.

Pillar, Michele. *Reign on Me* and *Look Who Loves You Now*.

Smith, Michael W. *Project*, *Friends*, and *Michael W. Smith II*.

Talbot, John Michael. *Be Exalted*, *Heart of the Shepherd*, *The Painter*, and *Come to the Quiet*.

White Heart. *Read the Book (Don't Wait for the Movie)*.

Miscellaneous Themes

"Be Good to Yourself." *Raised on Radio*. Journey.

"Forever Young." *Out of Order*. Rod Stewart.

"Glory of Love." *Solitude/Solitaire*. Peter Cetera.

"Greatest Love of All." *Whitney Houston*. Whitney Houston.

"Hip to Be Square." *Fore!* Huey Lewis and the News.

"Kyrie." *Welcome to the Real World*. Mr. Mister.

"Land of Confusion." *Invisible Touch*. Genesis.

"Lean on Me." *Life, Love, Pain*. Club Nouveau.

"Love Is the Answer." *The Best of England Dan and John Ford Coley*. England Dan and John Ford Coley.

"No One Is to Blame." *Action Replay*. Howard Jones.

"Put a Little Love in Your Heart." *Scrooged* (movie soundtrack). Annie Lennox and Al Green.

"Sanctify Yourself." *Once upon a Time*. Simple Minds.

"That's What Friends Are For." *Friends*. Dionne Warwick and Friends.

"When the Going Gets Tough the Tough Get Going." *Love Zone*. Billy Ocean.

"Wind Beneath My Wings." *Beaches* (movie soundtrack). Bette Midler.

"Without Your Love." *Best Bits*. Roger Daltrey.

Note: In order to stay more aware of the songs that the teenaged retreatants listen to, contact Don Kimball at Cornerstone Media, P.O. Box 6236, Santa Rosa, CA 95406; phone 707-542-TAPE. Cornerstone regularly publishes *Top Music Countdown*, a review of popular music, as well as songs adapted from current hits.

Appendix ▽

Eucharistic Liturgy Preparation

Chapter 6, "Lean on Me," provides the retreatants with the opportunity to participate in planning various aspects of the eucharistic liturgy: the decorations, the readings, the music, the offertory gifts, and the Prayer of the Faithful. During the time of the retreat schedule designated for liturgy preparation, the roles and the tasks of the planning committees are explained to the retreatants, who may then choose a committee to join. A staff member is assigned to assist each committee with its responsibilities. What follows are instructions for the liturgical preparation session, an explanation of each committee's work, and a planning sheet for eucharistic liturgy.

Instructions for the Liturgy Preparation Session

Staff: a liturgical coordinator and five people, one for each committee, to assist the committees in preparing their parts of the liturgy—readings, music, offertory gifts, Prayer of the Faithful, and decorations

Materials needed: ten Bibles, index cards, pencils, music books, and decoration supplies (crayons, scissors, glue, tape, construction paper, pencils, rulers, and butcher paper), and the planning sheet for eucharistic liturgy on page 121

Description of activities

1. Introduction: Introduce the activities for planning the liturgy saying something like the following: "This is the time that we have set aside to prepare for our closing liturgy. In this liturgy we will gather as a faith community to celebrate the presence of Jesus among us.

"Before we begin our planning, I would like to briefly review the main parts of the liturgy. Each eucharistic liturgy begins with a penitential rite. This is a time for us to reconcile with God and one another and to prepare ourselves to better listen to and respond to the Word of God.

"The eucharistic liturgy is then divided into two basic parts: the liturgy of the Word and the liturgy of the Eucharist.

"During the liturgy of the Word our focus is on *listening*. The Word of God is proclaimed in the readings from the Scriptures. A homily is given to help us to direct the message of Jesus to our daily life. After hearing the Word of God, we respond with the Prayer of the Faithful.

"During the liturgy of the Eucharist, our focus is on *sharing*. We prepare the offertory gifts, which are a spiritual expression of our very selves. We then recall the night before Jesus died, and we share in the Bread of Life. After the reception of Communion, the celebrant prays that we might be nourished by the Gift that we have received. And during the concluding rite, we are all sent to do the works of the Lord while praising and blessing God.

"I like to take the time to explain the various parts, because I believe that many people simply never learned what is happening during the eucharistic liturgy. My hope is that you will approach our closing liturgy with fresh eyes and ears. Let the words of the celebrant and the prayers become your own."

2. Committees: Explain that in order to help the retreatants participate more fully in this celebration, they will be responsible for various aspects of the liturgy. Five committees will be needed to plan the liturgy. Tell the retreatants to consider their interests and talents, and in light of those, to choose a committee they would like to help. The committees are decorations, music, offertory gifts, Prayer of the Faithful, and readings. Describe the responsibilities of each of these committees.

Explain that a limited number of people may serve on each committee. Ask the retreatants to raise their hands for the committee of their choice. Assign them to committees, trying to respect their choice as well as balancing the number for each committee. State how much time is available for the committee to work until the next activity and ask the committees to go to their respective locations and begin working.

The liturgy coordinator needs to be in touch with each committee as they are planning and to serve as a liaison among them. It will be important that all committees have a common theme in mind when carrying out their roles and tasks. Finally, the coordinator receives the information from each committee and completes the planning sheet for the eucharistic liturgy.

The Work of the Committees

Decorations Committee

This committee is responsible for preparing decorations for the liturgy. The decorations can contribute visibly to the whole environment and the whole action. They communicate like silent voices. The decorations are to be used to remind the participants of their reason for coming together.

Responsibilities
1. Use brainstorming to elicit ideas for decorations.
2. Decide upon an approach.
3. Prepare the decorations.
4. Choose a retreatant to explain each poster or decoration at the liturgy and to write the explanation on an index card.
5. On an index card, write the name of the person who will explain the posters or decorations and give it to the liturgical coordinator.
6. On the day of the liturgy, arrange the decorations.

Materials needed: crayons, scissors, glue, pencils, butcher paper, construction paper, and index cards

Suggested images
- Lent theme: Jesus, followers, people helping others, a cross, purple cloth
- Discipleship theme: family, clergy, religious community, single people helping others, the Holy Spirit, Mary and Jesus
- Substance-abuse prevention theme: Jesus, two roads, a person alone, communal praying, a sign that reads No Drugs
- Parent-teen theme: family figures, a heart, people talking with each other
- Graduation theme: a winding road, footprints with retreatants' names printed on them, friends walking hand in hand
- Advent theme: candles, a Christmas star, a wreath, a manger scene, Mary and Joseph traveling

Readings Committee

This committee is responsible for choosing and proclaiming the scriptural readings. The sacred Scriptures are central in the celebration of the liturgy. We are nourished by the Word of God. Care should be taken that the Word is proclaimed in such a way that the faithful will hear and understand: the one proclaiming the Word should stand, speak slowly, and read with expression. *(Note:* The committee may choose to reenact the readings by way of a skit.)

A brief introduction is given by a retreatant before each reading. A few minutes of silent reflection follow each reading.

Responsibilities
1. Use the list of suggested readings below for selecting readings that fit the theme of this retreat.
2. Choose the readings: the first reading, the second reading (optional), and the Gospel. (The first reading is usually taken from the Jewish Scriptures; the second reading is usually taken from the Epistles in the Christian Scriptures. A nonscriptural reading may be chosen for the second reading.) The music committee will plan the psalm response if it is to be sung.
3. Write the brief introductions to precede each reading.
4. Choose retreatants to introduce and proclaim the readings.
5. Write the list of the chosen readings and the names of the persons proclaiming each reading on an index card and give the card to the liturgical coordinator.
6. Before the liturgy, the retreatants who will proclaim the readings should rehearse. A staff

member should listen for the proper volume and speed and give feedback. Retreatants should stand while rehearsing the readings.

Materials needed: Bibles, index cards, and pencils

Form suggestions: The first and second readings begin with "A reading from . . ." and end with "This is the Word of the Lord." The gospel reading begins with "A reading from the holy Gospel according to . . ." and ends with "This is the Gospel of the Lord."

Suggested readings

Jewish Scriptures
Exod. 34:8–11 (Mount Sinai)
Jth. 9:11–12 (God as helper)
Sir. 42:15–25 (God's glory in nature)
Isa. 9:1–6 (A child is born.)
Ezek. 37:11–16 (shepherd)
Ezek. 37:1–14 (a new spirit)

Epistles
2 Cor. 13:11–13 (harmony and peace)
Eph. 4:11–16 (whole body)
2 Tim. 1:9–14 (holy life)
Titus 2:11–14 (awaiting Jesus)
Heb. 13:1–2,6,20–21 (blessing)
1 Pet. 5:5–11 (strengthening)

Gospels
Matt. 21:28–32 (the parable of two sons)
Matt. 18:10–14 (straying sheep)
Mark 1:2–8 (John the Baptist)
Mark 4:1–20 (the parable of the seed)
Luke 1:46–55 (Mary's canticle)
Luke 5:27–32 (the call of Levi)
John 13:1–17 (washing of the feet)

Music Committee

This committee is responsible for choosing the songs, leading the singing, and—if there is musical talent among them—providing instrumental accompaniment. The music is meant to provide an atmosphere of prayerful celebration. The music should be used to educate the retreatants and enhance the liturgy, not to entertain.

In planning the music, the following must be considered: (*a*) the message or theme of the readings, (*b*) the personality of the worship community, (*c*) the potential resources (including the competence and experience of the musicians), and (*d*) aesthetic balance and beauty.

The parts of the liturgy where music might be used are the following:
- entrance procession
- responsorial psalm
- gospel acclamation
- offertory procession (instrumental)
- Holy, Holy, Holy Lord
- memorial acclamation
- Great Amen
- Lord's Prayer
- Lamb of God
- Communion
- communion meditation
- recessional

Responsibilities
1. Use brainstorming with the following questions: What songs do you know? Will the accompaniment be by a staff member or a retreatant? What instruments will be used? Who is willing to sing (solo or as part of a choir)?
2. Choose appropriate songs for the different parts of the liturgy. (Not all areas need a song. If the group is relatively small, usually a communion meditation song is not needed with a communion song. One seems to be adequate.)
3. Write the list of songs to be used on an index card and give it to the liturgical coordinator.
4. Decide who will introduce the songs, who will be responsible for operating the tape player if needed, and who will rehearse the songs with the retreatants.
5. Practice the songs as a committee.
6. Before the liturgy starts, pass out the songbooks and rehearse the songs with the other retreatants.

Materials needed: songbooks, paper, pencils, index cards, a tape or a record player, tapes or records with the chosen songs, and instruments (if retreatants or staff members will be playing for the liturgy)

Suggested Music
(from volume 2 of *Glory and Praise* [Phoenix, AZ: North American Liturgy Resources, 1980] and *Praise and Worship Collection* [Maranatha! Music, 1987])
- "Remember Your Love" (Psalm 27), *Glory and Praise*
- "Lord Send Out Your Spirit" (Psalm 104), *Glory and Praise*
- "The Cry of the Poor" (Psalm 34), *Glory and Praise*
- "We Praise You" (Psalm 128), *Glory and Praise*
- "Seek Ye First" (Psalm 27), *Praise and Worship Collection*
- "Thy Word" (Psalm 119), *Praise and Worship Collection*

Committee for Offertory Gifts

This committee is responsible for choosing, explaining, and presenting the offertory gifts. The gifts, in addition to the bread and wine, are symbolic expressions of the people's entering into the sacrifice of Christ.

The gifts are prepared and presented in some order of significance. As each gift is presented, an explanation of the meaning of the gift is given.

Responsibilities
1. Use brainstorming with the following question: What gifts would symbolize the retreat experience or the retreatants themselves?
2. Decide on the gifts to be offered.
3. Write the appropriate explanations of the gifts to be offered.
4. Decide who will present the individual gifts, in what order they will be presented, and who is to give the explanations.
5. On an index card, write the names of the persons presenting the gifts and give the list to the liturgical coordinator.
6. Before the liturgy, place the gifts with the bread and the wine at the back of the chapel.

Materials needed: index cards, pencils, bread, and wine

Suggested gifts: flowers, a candle, a class ring, a volleyball

Suggested explanations

"We offer this bread, gift of the earth, which we shall eat and which will soon be transformed into the body of Jesus Christ."

"We offer this wine, fruit of the earth, which we shall drink and which will soon be transformed into the blood of Jesus Christ."

Committee for the Prayer of the Faithful

This committee is responsible for writing and presenting the Prayer of the Faithful. The Prayer of the Faithful is the action that ends the liturgy of the Word. As a response to having heard the message of the Lord, we respond as children of God in trust.

This prayer is intended to unite us with the individuals with whom we worship, as well as with people throughout the world. The petitions that are included in it usually focus on the needs of our civil and church leaders, the sick and the suffering, and the poor. There is also opportunity to pray for our own special intentions.

Responsibilities
1. Use brainstorming to elicit possible petitions.
2. Write the petitions.
3. Choose an appropriate form and response (e.g., "For . . . , let us pray to the Lord. Lord, hear us").
4. Decide upon the order in which the intentions will be offered.
5. On an index card, write the petitions along with the names of the persons offering them and give the card to the liturgical coordinator.

Materials needed: index cards and pencils

Planning Sheet for Eucharistic Liturgy

Theme: _____ **Date:** _____

Decorations: _____ explained by _____

Musical accompaniment: _____

Leader of song: _____

Introduction: read by _____ read by _____

Opening song: _____

First reading: introduced by _____ proclaimed by _____

Responsorial Psalm: _____ antiphon _____

_____ said ____ sung ____

Second reading: introduced by _____ proclaimed by _____

Gospel acclamation: _____

_____ said ____ sung ____

Gospel: introduced by _____ proclaimed by _____

Prayer of the Faithful: composed by _____ read by _____

Offertory song: _____

Offertory gifts: _____

presented by _____ explained by _____

Holy, Holy, Holy Lord: said ____ sung ____ version (if sung) _____

Memorial acclamation: _____

_____

Amen: said ____ sung ____ version (if sung) _____

Lord's Prayer: said ____ sung ____ version (if sung) _____

Lamb of God: said ____ sung ____ version (if sung) _____

Eucharistic ministers: _____

Communion song: _____

Communion meditation (if any): reading _____ read by _____

song _____

Recessional song: _____

Handout A: Permission to reproduce this handout is granted.

Acknowledgments ▽

I wish to thank the following people for their assistance in preparing the programs in this book:
- Emily Nabholz, SCN, president of the Sisters of Charity of Nazareth, Kentucky. Since 1981, Emily has been an inspiration to me—spiritually, professionally, and personally. She has significantly influenced my development in living a holistic lifestyle.
- Rose Ann Eaton, SP, pastoral minister, Saint Clement Church, Booneville, Indiana. Rose Ann introduced me to spiritual direction in 1977. Since then she has supported me as friend and spiritual companion.
- Cathy Mann, high school special education teacher; manager of counseling and testing, SOI Counseling and Testing Center, Manhattan Beach, California. Cathy provided information used in the camping retreat (chapter 10) and music resources used throughout this manual.
- Mark Mitchell, licensed marriage, family, and child counselor and adolescent drug and alcohol abuse counselor. Mark provided information used in the drug and alcohol abuse prevention retreat (chapter 8).
- Debbi and Gary Roehl, youth ministers, American Martyrs Church, Manhattan Beach, California. Debbi and Gary provided information used in the camping retreat (chapter 10) and music resources used throughout this manual.

I wish also to acknowledge the following permissions to use material previously published or authorized.

Unless noted otherwise, the scriptural excerpts in this manual are from the New American Bible. Copyrighted © 1970 by the Catholic Press and the Confraternity of Christian Doctrine, Washington, D.C.

The scriptural excerpts on pages 21, 34, 64, and 83 are from *Psalms Anew,* compiled by Nancy Schreck and Maureen Leach, pages 27, 120–121, 16, and 40 respectively. Copyright © by Saint Mary's Press, 1986. Used with permission.

The excerpt on page 42 is from *Words to Love By...,* by Mother Teresa (Notre Dame, IN: Ave Maria Press, 1983), page 47. Used with permission.

The icebreakers on pages 46–47 and 67 are from *More New Games,* by Andrew Fluegelman. Copyright © 1981 by Headlands Press, Inc. Reprinted by permission of Doubleday, a division of Bantam, Doubleday, Dell Publishing Group, Inc.

The icebreakers on pages 53–54 are from *Playfair: Everybody's Guide to Noncompetitive Play.* Copyright © 1980 by Matt Weinstein and Joel Goodman. Reproduced for Saint Mary's Press by permission of Impact Publishers, Inc., P.O. Box 1094 San Luis Obispo, CA 93406. Further reproduction prohibited.

The reconciliation service on pages 60–61 is adapted from *Today's Missal,* vol. 54, no. 3: 52. Used with permission.

The "Communal Prayer of Contrition" on page 60 is excerpted from the English translation of *The Roman Missal* © 1973, International Committee on English in the Liturgy, Inc. All rights reserved. Used with permission.

The guided relaxation exercise on pages 69–70 is adapted from pages 33–34 of *Guide to Stress Reduction,* © 1980, 1985 by L. John Mason, M.D. Published by Celestial Arts, Berkeley, California.

The excerpt on page 82 is from *Wellsprings: A Book of Spiritual Exercises,* by Anthony de Mello (Garden City, NY: Doubleday and Co., 1985), pages 148–149. Copyright © Gujarat Sahitya Prakash, Anand, India. Used with permission.

The excerpts on pages 85, 88, 92, 97, 99, and 101 are from *Prayers for the Domestic Church,* by Edward M. Hays (Easton, KS: Forest of Peace Books, 1979), pages 51, 44, 35, 37, 58, and 163 respectively. Used with permission.

Psalm 67 on page 106 is adapted and reprinted from *Psalms/Now,* by Leslie F. Brandt, page 107. Copyright © 1973 Concordia Publishing House, Saint Louis, Missouri. Reprinted by permission of CPH.

Photo Credits
James Shaffer: cover; pages 9, 51, 75, 89, 103
Steve and Mary Skjold: pages 29, 89
Cleo Freelance: page 29